Student Activities Manual
to accompany

¡Saludos!
Introductory Spanish

Student Activities Manual
to accompany

¡Saludos!
Introductory Spanish

Oscar Ozete

University of Southern Indiana

Prepared by
David Stillman

THOMSON

™

HEINLE

Australia Canada Mexico Singapore Spain United Kingdom United States

¡Saludos! Student Activities Manual
Oscar Ozete

Printed in the United States of America
  4 5 6 7 8 9 10   06 05 04

For more information contact Heinle, 25 Thomson Place, Boston, MA 02210 USA,
or you can visit our Internet site at http://www.heinle.com

For permission to use material from this text or product contact us:
Tel   1-800-730-2214
Fax   1-800-730-2215
Web   www.thomsonrights.com

ISBN: 0-03-026739-0

Contents

Preface   vi

Workbook   1

Laboratory Manual   83

Preface

This *Student Activities Manual* is designed to accompany *¡Saludos!: Introductory Spanish.* It is actually two books in one: the Workbook and the Laboratory Manual. Both components are coordinated chapter by chapter with the main textbook and are intended to review, reinforce, and enrich the vocabulary, grammatical points, and cultural background presented in *¡Saludos!* The answers to the exercises are to be found in the answer key at the end of the manual.

This manual contains a wide variety of communicative and more traditional written activities. The successful completion of these workbook exercises is a key step in mastery of writing at this level of study of the Spanish language. The exercises proceed in difficulty from closed activities emphasizing specific vocabulary and grammatical structures at the beginning of each chapter to compositions and translations at the end of the chapter.

The *Laboratory Manual* provides practice in listening comprehension, speaking, and pronunciation. It is designed to be used in conjunction with the audio program of *¡Saludos!* Within each section, the exercises are graded for level of difficulty in listening and speaking practice. The voices on the recordings are from a variety of native speakers from different countries. The complete tapescript is available upon request from the publisher.

The authors would like to thank Jeff Gilbreath and Jason Krieger of Harcourt College Publishers for their efforts in editing this material; we sincerely appreciate their assistance and insightful comments.

Oscar Ozete
David Stillman

Workbook

Lección preliminar
¡Saludos!

Conversación ·

A. Fill in the missing words. This conversation is between two friends and is therefore in the **tú** form.

Fernando: Hola, Miguel. Buenas _____.

Miguel: _____ tardes, Fernando. ¿_____ tal?

Fernando: Bien, _____. ¿Cómo _____ tú?

Miguel: Más o _____.

Fernando: Huy, _____ tarde. Perdón.

Miguel: _____ luego, Fernando.

B. Fill in the missing words. This conversation is between a professor and a student and is therefore in the **Ud.** form.

Señora Ochoa: Buenos _____, señorita Soto.

Señorita Soto: Ah, _____ Ochoa. ¿Cómo _____ Ud.?

Señora Ochoa: _____ bastante bien, gracias. ¿_____ Ud.?

Señorita Soto: Yo estoy _____.

Señora Ochoa: Perdón, señorita. Es _____. Adiós.

Señorita Soto: Ah, sí. Adiós, señora.

Cultura ·

A. Read the following passage. Then reread it and fill in the blanks with the best of the answers suggested in parentheses. Note the meaning of these words: **hay** (there is, there are) and **suroeste** (southwest).

La influencia hispánica es muy importante en los Estados Unidos. En muchas (1) _____

(capitales, países, ciudades) hay comunidades hispanas muy grandes, como en Nueva York, Chicago, Dallas,

Houston, Miami, San Diego y Los Ángeles. La mayor parte de los (2) _____ (hispanos, nortea-

mericanos, españoles) son de origen mexicano, puertorriqueño o cubano, pero hay hispanos de todos los (3)

_____ (días, países, estados) de Hispanoamérica.

La influencia hispania es muy importante en el suroeste de los Estados Unidos, la parte del país que era[1]

territorio (4) _____ (cubano, mexicano, norteamericano) antes de la guerra con México

[1] was

(1846–1848). Varios nombres de estados son de origen español: California, Nevada y (5) _____

(Nueva York, la Florida, Michigan). ¿Conocen Uds. (6) _____ (los residentes, las tradiciones, las

palabras) en español del *Wild West:* rodeo, pinto y bronco?

Alfabeto . . . .

A. Write the letter that corresponds to each letter name.

1. efe _____

2. jota _____

3. ka _____

4. eñe _____

5. i griega _____

6. uve _____

7. elle _____

8. zeta _____

9. hache _____

10. doble ve _____

B. Write the letters that make up the names.

MODELO•••➤ Juan ➜ jota-u-a-ene

1. Hugo _____

2. Laura _____

3. Pablo _____

4. Vera _____

5. Yolanda _____

Números 0–99 . . . .

A. Write out the amount in pesos.

MODELO•••➤ $35 ➜ treinta y cinco pesos

1. $59 _____

2. $22 _____

3. $84 _____

4. $67 _____

5. $18 _____

6. $13 _____

7. $36 _____

8. $45 _____

9. $78 _____

10. $90 _____

Expresiones para la clase..........................

A. Circle the correct completion for each sentence.

1. Me hace el favor de (abrir, preguntarle) el libro.

2. Me hace el favor de (repetir, cerrar) el cuaderno.

3. ¿(Cómo, Cuál) es el número de Pedro Ochoa?

4. San Diego es (una ciudad, un estado) de los Estados Unidos.

¿Cómo se dice?...................................

A. Circle the correct completion(s) for each sentence so that it (they) expresses (express) the meaning indicated.

1. You want someone to read an e-mail message.

   Me hace el favor de (leer, escribir) (la página Web, el correo electrónico).

2. You want to tell someone it's late. You say:

   (Está, Es) tarde.

3. You suggest to your friend Marta that you and she both listen.

   (Vamos a, Me hace el favor de) escuchar.

4. You want to tell a friend that Spanish is the language used in Guatemala.

   En Guatemala (son, hablan) español.

Orígenes ....

A. Choose words from the following list to complete the sentences below correctly. Remember to distinguish between males (forms ending in **-o**) and females (forms ending in **-a**).

Masculine forms	**Feminine forms**
cubano	cubana
mexicano	mexicana
norteamericano	norteamericana
puertorriqueño	puertorriqueña

4

1. María es de San Juan, Puerto Rico. María es _____.

2. Larry es de Wáshington. Larry es _____.

3. El chico es de Cuba. El chico es _____.

4. Norma es de los Estados Unidos. La chica es _____.

5. Raúl es de México. Raúl es _____.

6. Ana es de Cuba. Ana es _____.

Vamos a leer (y a escribir) . . . .

A. Look at the following ad for sneakers taken from the Spanish edition of the *Miami Herald*.

1. Write out the three prices given in the ad. Notice that Spanish reads these prices as two pairs of numbers, just as English does: $12.79 = doce setenta y nueve.

   $14.99 _____

   $15.99 _____

   $19.99 _____

2. ¿Cuál es el número de teléfono de Lorraine athletic force, Inc.? (Write out the number.)

   Es el _____

   _____

Vamos a explorar el ciberespacio . . . .

Using the World Wide Web as a resource to learn Spanish. The World Wide Web offers many fascinating sites throughout the Spanish-speaking world dealing with the cultural topics in this lesson. Take a virtual field trip. Go to http://www.harcourtcollege.com/spanish/saludosrecuerdos to discover more.

Lección 1
La clase y las presentaciones

Conversación . . . .

A. En la clase. Two students meet each other on the first day of class. Complete their conversation.

José Luis: Buenos días. ¿ _____ te llamas?

Felisa: _____ Felisa Camacho. ¿Y _____?

José Luis: Me llamo _____ Peña.

Felisa: Mucho _____, José Luis,

José Luis: El _____ es _____, Felisa.

B. En la oficina. Two employees of a big company meet. Complete their conversation.

Marcos Lares: Buenos días. _____ llamo Marcos Lares. _____ ingeniero. ¿Cómo

_____ _____ Ud., señorita?

Elena Soto: Buenos días. Yo _____ _____ Elena Soto. _____ programadora.

Marcos Lares: _____, señorita.

Elena Soto: _____.

Sujetos . . . .

A. *Tú* vs. *Ud.* Check which question you would use to find out where the following people are from.

	¿De dónde eres?	¿De dónde es Ud.?
1. your brother	_____	_____
2. a professor	_____	_____
3. a school secretary	_____	_____
4. a child	_____	_____
5. your friend's father	_____	_____

Pronombres . . . .

A. Which pronoun would you use if you were talking about these people?

1. yourself _____

2. a girlfriend _____

6

3. your friend Miguel _____

4. two new female students _____

5. yourself and your friend José _____

B. Complete the following sentences with the missing subject pronouns.

1. ¿ _____ eres de Colombia? ¡ _____ soy de Colombia también!

2. José y Teresa Lara son profesores. _____ es profesor de español y _____ es profesora de inglés.

3. —¿De dónde son Rafael y Pedro? ¿De Venezuela?

—No, de Venezuela, no. _____ son de Guatemala. Amalia y Laura son de Venezuela.

4. Luis y Tomás, ¿ _____ son ingenieros? _____ somos ingenieras también.

El verbo ser ···

A. **¿Qué son y de dónde son?** Use the verb **ser** to write out what each of the people indicated does and where he or she is from.

MODELO• • • ➤ Luis/deportista/Colombia ➜ Luis es deportista. Es de Colombia.

1. yo/estudiante/los Estados Unidos

_____

2. la señora Morales/profesora/Venezuela

_____

3. Carlos y yo/actores/España

_____

4. tú/escritor/Cuba

_____

5. ustedes/licenciados/Puerto Rico

_____

6. Mauricio/cantante/México

_____

7. usted/abogada/Guatemala

_____

8. Rosa y Pedro/directores/Chile

_____

En el salón de clase

A. Write the Spanish word for each of these items. Include the definite article.

1. backpack (#15)

_____

2. chair (#7)

_____

3. pencil (#12)

_____

4. calculator (#18)

_____

5. students (#21)

_____

6. light (#3)

_____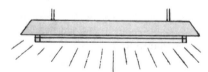

7. chalkboard (#5)

_____

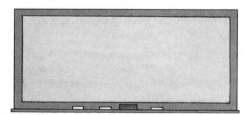

8. books (#8)

_____

Sustantivos y artículos . . . .

A. La escuela de Juanito. Juanito Oñate has just returned from his first day at school and is telling his parents about his classroom. To find out what Juanito says, complete the following sentences with the appropriate indefinite article.

MODELO● ● ● ➤   Hay __una__ pizarra.

1. Hay _____ televisor.

2. Hay _____ computadoras.

3. Hay _____ chicos.

4. Hay _____ mesas.

5. Hay _____ reloj.

6. Hay _____ videocasetera.

B. Me gusta(n). Write **Me gusta(n)** or **No me gusta(n)** and the appropriate definite article to say whether or not you like these items.

1. _____ clases.

2. _____ libro de español.

3. _____ ciudad.

4. _____ computadoras.

5. _____ videos.

6. _____ béisbol.

7. _____ mapa.

8. _____ deportes.

C. Gusto. Use the cues given to create conversations between people about what they like and don't like. Follow the model and use the definite article before the nouns.

MODELOS● ● ● ➤   libro/sí ➜
          —¿Te gusta el libro?
          —Sí, me gusta.
          libro/no ➜
          —¿Te gusta e libro?
          —No, no me gusta.

1. lecciones/sí

— _____

— _____

2. reloj/no

— _____

— _____

3. cantantes (masc.)/no

— _____

— _____

4. baloncesto/sí

— _____

— _____

5. computadora/no

— _____

— _____

Vamos a leer. . . . .

A. Look at the following ad from the Spanish edition of the *Miami Herald (Nuevo Herald)*. Skim the ad looking for the following information:

1. What is the ad for?

2. Are the services offered for adults only?

3. Is there something to cut out in the ad?

Now read the ad carefully and answer the following questions. Write down any words from the ad that you base your answer on.

4. Where is the instructor from?

_____

5. Can you find the Spanish word for "children" in the ad? Hint: Find the words that tell who can enroll in this program.

_____

6. Find the following Spanish words:

coupon _____

free _____

7. This instruction is supposed to develop many personal qualities in the students. Find the Spanish words for:

discipline _____

respect _____

excellence _____

self-confidence _____

8. What can you get with the coupon?

_____

Vamos a escribir . . . .

A. **Correo electrónico en español** (E-mail in Spanish). You have just been given the e-mail address of a student in Mexico. Write your introductory e-mail to your new Mexican pen pal. Include the following elements:

1. Introduce yourself and tell where you are from.
2. Ask the Mexican student his or her name.
3. Tell three or four things you like and then ask if your pen pal likes school (use **la universidad**) and sports.
4. Sign off using the name of this book (*¡Saludos!*).

Write your e-mail:

_____

_____

_____

_____

_____

_____

_____

_____

_____

_____

_____

Vamos a explorar el ciberespacio . . . .

Sports in the Hispanic World. The World Wide Web offers many fascinating sites throughout the Spanish-speaking world dealing with the cultural topics in this lesson. Take a virtual field trip. Go to http://www.harcourtcollege.com/spanish/saludosrecuerdos to discover more.

Lección 2
La familia y las descripciones
La familia . . . .

A. La familia de Javier Rojo. Read the following passage in which Javier Rojo describes his family. Then reread it and fill in the blanks with the best of the answers suggested in parentheses.

¡Hola! Me _____ (1. hablo, llamo, contesto) Javier Rojo. (2. Soy, Es, Eres) soltero.

_____ (3. Deseo, Manejo, Estudio) en la universidad. Tomo _____ (4. clases, estu-

diantes, libros) de historia y de ciencias políticas. Me _____ (5. gusto, gustan, gusta) la historia

de Europa. Por eso estudio francés y español. Necesito _____ (6. enseñar, participar, hablar)

alemán también.

Yo vivo *(live)* con mi familia. En mi familia, _____ (7. son, soy, somos) seis: mis padres, mi

abuela Teresa, mi hermano Carlos, mi hermana Alejandra y yo. Mi hermano Carlos _____ (8.

está, son, es) serio y trabajador. Mi hermana es inteligente y sociable. Mis hermanos estudian en

_____ (9. la oficina, el país, la universidad) también. Sus clases son _____ (10. pere-

zosas, interesantes, altas), pero muy difíciles.

B. Mi familia y yo. Write a brief description of your family and yourself in Spanish. Tell who the members of the family are, what their names are, and what they are like. You can also tell where people are from and what their professions are.

_____

_____

_____

_____

_____

_____

_____

_____

_____

_____

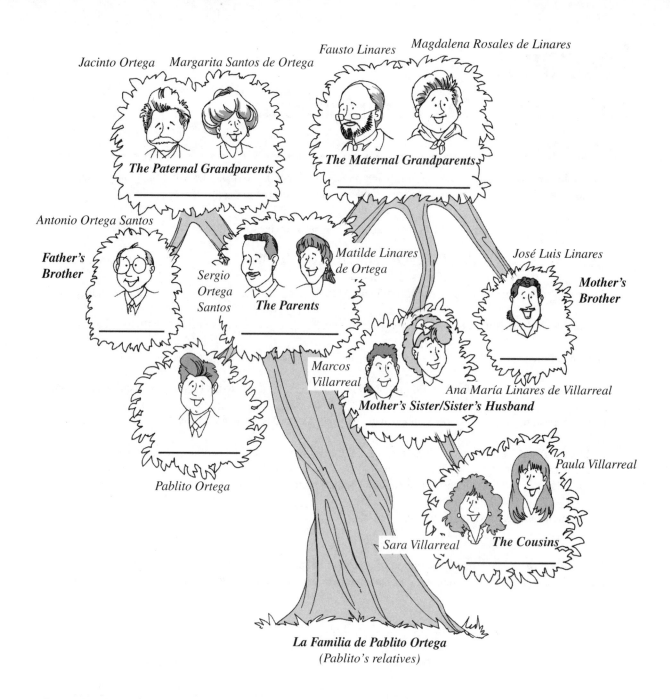

Jacinto Ortega Margarita Santos de Ortega

Fausto Linares Magdalena Rosales de Linares

The Paternal Grandparents

The Maternal Grandparents

Antonio Ortega Santos

Father's Brother

Sergio Ortega Santos

Matilde Linares de Ortega

The Parents

José Luis Linares

Mother's Brother

Marcos Villarreal

Pablito Ortega

Ana María Linares de Villarreal

Mother's Sister/Sister's Husband

Paula Villarreal

Sara Villarreal **The Cousins**

La Familia de Pablito Ortega
(Pablito's relatives)

C. La familia de Pablito Ortega. Complete the terms for the members of Pablito's family.

Las descripciones ....

A. Mis asociaciones. Try some quick associations in Spanish. Pick three adjectives that occur to you to describe each of the nouns below. Make sure your associations agree in gender and number with the noun. A list of adjectives is provided to jog your memory if necessary.

MODELO•••➤ la profesora: trabajadora, graciosa, dinámica

Adjetivos alto/bajo/fuerte/débil/divertido/aburrido/inteligente/tonto/mejor/peor/nuevo/viejo/joven/ordenado/desordenado/rico/pobre/simpático/antipático/trabajador/perezoso/fácil/difícil/rubio/guapo/bonito/moreno/feo/triste/excelente/grande/pequeño/delgado/gordo

1. los estudiantes _____

2. la universidad _____

3. mi novio (mi novia) _____

4. la biblioteca _____

5. mi familia _____

6. mis clases _____

7. los amigos _____

B. Busco novio(a). Write a personal ad you could place in the campus paper. Describe yourself **(Soy...)** and the person you are looking for **(Busco un chico/una chica...).** Write 3–5 adjectives for yourself and the person of your dreams.

_____

_____

_____

_____

_____

_____

_____

El presente de los verbos regulares en -ar ....

A. According to the context, complete the activity each person does by putting the appropriate verb in the correct form.

MODELO•••➤ (manejar, estudiar, ayudar) Yo __estudio__ en la biblioteca.

1. (esperar, mirar, trabajar)   Mi padre _____ en una oficina.

2. (enseñar, participar, buscar)   El profesor Sánchez _____ muy bien.

3. (mirar, dar, necesitar)   ¿Qué _____ tú comprar?

4. (descansar, bailar, visitar)   Los turistas _____ la ciudad.

5. (cocinar, escuchar, usar)   El profesor habla y nosotros _____ .

6. (tomar, practicar, caminar)   Yo _____ té en la cafetería.

B. **Mi día.** Use the following verbs to describe a typical day of yours. Put them in the order that reflects your activities and write them in the **yo** form.

estudiar	caminar a la universidad (a la oficina)
desayunar	preparar las lecciones
descansar	regresar a mi casa
escuchar en las clases	mirar televisión

1. _____

2. _____

3. _____

4. _____

5. _____

6. _____

7. _____

8. _____

El verbo estar . . . .

A. **¿Cómo están y dónde están?** Tell how these people are feeling and where they are in two sentences. Use the verb **estar** and make adjectives agree with the person they refer to.

MODELO• • • ➤   Mónica/enamorado/su casa   ➔   Mónica está enamorada. Está en su casa.

1. yo (woman)/cansado/gimnasio

_____

2. Marcos y Francisco/entusiasmado/aquí

_____

3. Alfredo y yo/ocupado/oficina

_____

4. Marta y Raquel/callado/clase

_____

5. (talking to Isabel) tú/aburrido/biblioteca

_____

B. Los gemelos *(twins)*. Complete this description of the twins Javier and Jacinto by adding the correct form of **ser** or **estar,** as required.

1. Javier y Jacinto _____ hermanos. _____ mexicanos.

2. _____ guapos y muy simpáticos.

3. Los dos hermanos _____ inteligentes. _____ estudiantes.

4. Hoy _____ en la universidad.

5. Sus novias _____ Elena y Margarita. Ellas _____ en la universidad también.

6. Las chicas _____ muy entusiasmadas con sus clases. Ellas _____ muy trabajadoras.

7. Elena _____ muy enamorada de Javier. Margarita y Jacinto _____ muy enamorados también.

8. Los cuatro jóvenes _____ en la cafetería de la universidad.

9. Toman café y hablan de sus clases. _____ muy contentos.

10. La cafetería _____ muy grande y hay muchos estudiantes allí, pero Javier, Jacinto, Elena y

    Margarita _____ muy relajados allí.

Vamos a leer..........................

A. Here is an advertisement placed by a school in Bogotá, Colombia, in one of Colombia's most widely read newspapers, *El Tiempo.*

Skim the ad quickly and answer the following questions.

1. What kind of a school is this? _____

2. What foreign language is taught? _____

3. Can you find the sections for higher education (postsecondary school) and graduate studies? What words signal these sections?

_____

Now read the ad more carefully and answer these questions:

4. What is the name of the school? What geographic feature of Colombia is reflected in the name?

_____

5. What kind of careers does the school prepare you for in foreign languages? Can you find the Spanish word for translation?

_____

_____

6. What kind of engineering does the school teach?

_____

7. Which subjects can be studied both during the day and at night? What words communicate this?

_____

8. Look at the following vocabulary and the ad, and then answer the question below:

el contador	accountant	**la informática**	information processing, computers
el diseño	design	**la red**	net, network
la empresa	firm, company, business		

a. How do you say *business administration* in Spanish?

_____

b. How do you say *systems analysis and design* in Spanish?

_____

c. Which professionals can learn to use computers in their work? What program listed does this?

_____

Vamos a explorar el ciberespacio . . . .

The Family. The World Wide Web offers many fascinating sites throughout the Spanish-speaking world dealing with the cultural topics in this lesson. Take a virtual field trip. Go to http://www.harcourtcollege.com/spanish/saludosrecuerdos to discover more.

Lección 3
Las comidas

Conversación . . . .

A. Complete the following summary of the conversation found on page 76 of the textbook by filling in the missing words.

Sara es de los (1) _____, pero (2) _____ en México. Está en un

(3) _____ ahora con su amiga mexicana, Rosario. En el restaurante (4) ellas _____

unos chilaquiles muy (5) _____. Los chilaquiles son pedacitos de (6) _____

mexicana con salsa y (7) _____. Las dos chicas van a (8) _____ chilaquiles. Viene el

(9) _____ a la mesa. Rosario dice *(says)* que él es muy (10) _____.

Cultura. . . . .

A. Read the following passage. Then reread it and fill in the blanks with the best of the answers suggested in parentheses.

En el mundo hispánico la comida varía según la región, su clima y su geografía. En España, un país que

tiene muchas costas, (1) _____ (la fruta, el pescado, la sopa) es muy importante. Un plato es-

pañol muy famoso es (2) _____ (la paella, el mango, la empanada), que se prepara con arroz,

pollo y mariscos.

Hispanoamérica es muy grande, y tiene diferentes zonas climáticas. También hay mucha influencia

indígena en la comida. Muchas cosas que (3) _____ (sabemos, comemos, abrimos) ahora en los Es-

tados Unidos y en Europa como el maíz, el tomate, la papa y el pavo vienen de los indígenas de Hispanoamérica.

Los (4) _____ (plátanos, puercos, tacos) y las enchiladas son típicos de México, y la

comida mexicana es (5) _____ (guapa, típica, picante). Los argentinos comen mucha

(6) _____ (verdura, pasta, carne) asada porque el país tiene mucho ganado *(cattle)*. En el

Caribe hay (7) _____ (galletas, frutas, carnes) diferentes, como las naranjas, los limones, los

mangos, las papayas y el coco.

Ir . . . .

A. Create conversations in which you ask where these people are going and answer with the cues provided.

MODELO• • • ➤ tú/correo
—¿Adónde vas?
—Voy al correo.

1. Felipe/el cine

— _____

— _____

2. Los García/el mercado

— _____

— _____

3. Rosario/el restaurante

— _____

— _____

4. yo/la universidad

— _____

— _____

5. ustedes/la ciudad

— _____

— _____

6. el mesero/la mesa

— _____

— _____

Ir a + *infinitive* . . . .

A. **Planes.** Write five activities you are going to do this weekend. Then write five you believe your professor *isn't* going to do. Use the infinitives and phrases provided or others you already know.

MODELOS• • • ➤ Voy a visitar a mis amigos.
Mi profesor no va a jugar al fútbol.

asistir a un concierto	ir al cine/al teatro
comer en un restaurante	jugar al fútbol/al tenis/al béisbol
escuchar música	preparar una comida fantástica
estudiar	ver a mis amigos

Ud.

1. _____

2. _____

3. _____

4. _____

5. _____

Su profesor(a)

6. _____

7. _____

8. _____

9. _____

10. _____

El presente de los verbos *-er/-ir* . . . .

A. ¿Qué hacen? Write down what these people are doing. Choose the appropriate verb from the context and then write the correct form.

MODELO• • • ➤ Mis compañeros __leen__ el libro de español. (comer, leer)

1. Yo _____ la tarea. (escribir, vender)

2. Tú _____ estudiar. (comprender, deber)

3. Sara _____ mucho a la familia. (aprender, ver)

4. Nosotros _____ la puerta. (abrir, recibir)

5. Los nifños _____ (escribir, compartir) la comida.

6. Yo _____ un libro en español. (creer, leer)

7. ¿Por qué no _____ (tú) el vocabulario? (aprender, conocer)

8. Tú y yo _____ (comer, vivir) en un restaurante.

Las preguntas. . . . .

A. Marta is telling Juanito about his new school. To check what she tells him, he rephrases her statements as questions. Write Juanito's questions.

MODELO• • • ➤ Muchos estudiantes estudian en esta escuela.
¿Estudian muchos estudiantes en esta escuela?

1. Los estudiantes llegan temprano.

_____

2. Cada profesor enseña cinco clases.

_____

3. Los estudiantes leen muchos libros.

_____

4. La profesora Jiménez enseña español.

_____

B. Now Juanito isn't sure he has heard Marta's information. Have him ask the questions that would elicit the information he is not sure of.

MODELO• • • ➤   No hay clases *el lunes.*
¿Cuándo no hay clases?

1. Mis amigos estudian *en la biblioteca.*

_____

2. *El profesor Suárez* enseña biología.

_____

3. Voy *al cine* mañana.

_____

4. Isabel Morales es *de Venezuela.*

_____

La *a* personal . . . .

A. Marcos tells about his visit to his uncle and aunt in La Paz, Bolivia. Complete his story by adding personal **a** where necessary.

1. En julio siempre visito _____ mis tíos en La Paz.

2. Ya conozco muy bien _____ la ciudad.

3. Cuando estoy allí, veo _____ mis primos Eduardo y Clara.

4. Escucho _____ Clara cuando canta. Ella canta muy bien.

5. Con mi primo Eduardo, miro _____ muchos programas de televisión.

6. También buscamos _____ sus amigos para jugar fútbol.

Saber y conocer . . . .

A. Preguntas. Form questions about these things and people using **¿Sabes...?** or **¿Conoces...?** Remember to use personal **a** if needed.

MODELO• • • ➤   bailar ➜ ¿Sabes bailar?

1. el vocabulario _____

2. cocinar _____

3. la hermana de Mario _____

4. el nuevo restaurante mexicano _____

5. qué son los chilaquiles _____

6. de dónde es Lola Laredo _____

7. Puerto Rico _____

8. que José vive aquí _____

El tiempo

A. Los estudiantes internacionales. A group of international students is talking about the weather in their home countries. Complete each of their statements with two weather expressions.

1. Yo soy de Miami. En Miami en verano _____

_____

2. Yo soy de Londres, capital de Inglaterra. En Londres en noviembre _____

_____

3. Yo soy de Toronto, Canadá. En invierno en Toronto _____

_____

4. Yo soy de la ciudad de México. En mi ciudad en primavera _____

_____

Vamos a leer

A. Christmas is one of those holidays when people overeat, in Spain as well as in the United States. On the next page, read the recipe from the Spanish daily *ABC* for a soup that helps take off those unwanted pounds. Key words are **quemar** *(to burn)* and **grasa** *(fat)*.

Skim the ad quickly and answer the following questions in English.

1. Who has been consulted about this soup? _____

2. What is their opinion of it? _____

3. What food group is represented in the ingredients? _____

Now read the information more carefully and answer the questions that follow. Answer in Spanish those questions that are asked in Spanish.

4. ¿Cuántas cebollas debes poner en la sopa?

_____

5. ¿Cuántos tomates?

_____

Sopa para quemar grasa

Ingredientes

Seis cebollas grandes

Dos pimientos verdes

Medio kilo de tomates naturales

Una cabeza grande de repollo

Una pizca de sal

Una pizca de pimienta

Dos ramilletes grandes de apio

Un cubito de caldo de pollo (opcional)

Preparación

Cortar la verdura en trozos pequeños o medianos, ponerlos a hervir en agua y pasarlos por la batidora. La sopa se puede servir fría o caliente.

E. Segura/ABC

6. Can you find the following Spanish words?

pepper (as in green pepper) _____

a pinch (of salt or pepper) _____

celery _____

chicken broth _____

7. Look at the meaning of the following words and explain how the soup is prepared:

cortar	to cut	**la batidora**	blender
el trozo	piece	**mediano**	average
hervir	to boil	**pasarlos por**	to put them through

8. In what two ways can you serve the soup?

_____

Vamos a explorar el ciberespacio . . . .

Restaurants. The World Wide Web offers many fascinating sites throughout the Spanish-speaking world dealing with the cultural topics in this lesson. Take a virtual field trip. Go to http://www.harcourtcollege.com/spanish/saludosrecuerdos to discover more.

Lección 4
Las actividades diarias

Horario . . . .

A. Una estudiante universitaria. Look over Rafaela Zurita's class schedule and read the statements that follow. Indicate whether each statement is **C** *(cierto)* or **F** *(falso)*. Correct the false statements.

Horario   Rafaela Zurita   Universidad de Costa Rica

Hora	lunes	martes	miércoles	jueves	viernes
9:00	laboratorio de lenguas	física		física	
10:00			laboratorio de lenguas	inglés	
11:00	informática	literatura	informática	literatura	informática
12:00	almuerzo— cafetería	historia	almuerzo— cafetería	historia	almuerzo— cafetería
1:00	inglés	almuerzo— cafetería	inglés	almuerzo— cafetería	laboratorio de física
2:00	gimnasia	francés	gimnasia	francés	laboratorio de física
3:00	administración de empresas		administración de empresas		laboratorio de física
4:00					laboratorio de física

1. Rafaela almuerza a las doce todos los días.   C   F

2. Rafaela termina tarde los viernes.   C   F

3. Rafaela estudia inglés y francés.   C   F

4. Los lunes y los miércoles Rafaela va al laboratorio de física.   C   F

5. Rafaela tiene clase de administración de empresas tres veces por semana.   C   F

6. Las clases de informática son los lunes, miércoles y viernes.   C   F

7. Rafaela tiene clase de gimnasia los martes y los viernes.   C   F

8. Rafaela estudia historia y literatura.   C   F

Cultura . . . .

A. Contrast Latin American universities with American ones by completing the following sentences.

1. Los estudiantes norteamericanos van directamente a la universidad después de la escuela secundaria, pero

en algunos países en Hispanoamérica _____

_____

2. En las universidades norteamericanas los estudiantes tienen muchas opciones. Los estudiantes his-

panoamericanos _____

3. Las universidades norteamericanas son el centro de la vida social de los estudiantes. En Hispanoamérica,

la vida social _____

4. Las universidades norteamericanas tienen residencias. Las universidades hispanoamericanas _____

_____

5. Hay equipos deportivos en las universidades norteamericanas. En las universidades latinoamericanas ge-

neralmente _____

Los adjetivos posesivos. ·

A. . . Rewrite the sentences below, substituting the italicized word with the one in parentheses. Make all necessary changes.

> **MODELO** • • • ➤ Tus *fotos* son muy buenas. (carta)
> ➜ Tu carta es muy buena.

1. Nuestras *actividades* son interesantes. (clase)

_____

2. Mi *horario* es difícil. (tareas)

_____

3. Nuestra *profesora* es simpática. (amigos)

_____

4. Tu *trabajo* es importante. (reuniones)

_____

5. Aquí están sus *papeles*, señor. (horario)

_____

B. **La posesión.** A friend of yours finds a lot of things that people have left in the classroom. You tell him to whom they belong.

> **MODELO** • • • ➤ mochila/la estudiante Julia Pérez
> ➜ La mochila es de la estudiante Julia Pérez.

1. reloj/el profesor

_____

2. bolígrafo/el chico mexicano

_____

3. lápices/la amiga de Pedro

_____

4. cuadernos/los nuevos estudiantes

_____

5. papel/el muchacho español

_____

Actividades . . . .

A. Look at the grid and write sentences that tell what these people are doing or what they may do. Then write at least five sentences with the activities that are not checked. You decide who does them.

MODELO• • • ➤   cerrar la puerta/Mario ➜ Mario cierra la puerta.

	Mario	tú	los estudiantes	yo	mis amigos y yo
cerrar la puerta	√		√		√
almorzar en la universidad		√	√	√	
empezar la lección	√	√		√	√
poder estudiar química	√				
entender el manual	√		√	√	
volver a casa		√		√	√
dormir mucho					
jugar al baloncesto					
pensar mucho en los estudios					

Mario

_____

_____

_____

tú

_____

_____

_____

los estudiantes

_____

_____

_____

yo

_____

_____

_____

mis amigos y yo

_____

_____

_____

Additional sentences

_____

_____

_____

_____

_____

Verbos con cambios en el presente . . . .

A. Yo también. You want to do whatever your friends are doing. Say so by completing the following sentences beginning with **si** *(if)* with the correct forms of the verbs in parentheses.

MODELO•••➤ ➜ (jugar) Si tú *juegas* al fútbol, yo *juego* también.

1. (venir)   Si Juan _____ mañana, yo _____ también.

2. (salir)   Si Juan _____ de la biblioteca, yo _____ también.

3. (hacer)   Si Uds. _____ la tarea, yo _____ la tarea también.

4. (traer)   Si los otros _____ sus libros, yo _____ mis libros también.

5. (poner)   Si tu _____ el mantel, yo _____ los platos.

Los pronombres reflexivos . . . .

A. Un día típico. Help Andrés describe a typical day in his life by filling in the blanks with the present tense of the verb that best completes each sentence.

1. Cuando tengo clases, _____ (preocuparse, despertarse, llamarse) temprano.

2. No _____ en la cama. (quedarse, maquillarse, irse)

3. _____ en seguida. (acostarse, dormirse, levantarse)

4. _____ y me afeito. (ducharse, divertirse, quedarse)

5. Después, _____ la ropa y bajo a la cocina para desayunar. (secarse, lavarse, ponerse)

6. A las ocho y diez, _____. (dormirse, irse, despertarse)

7. Llego a la universidad y _____ a mis clases. (tomar, escuchar, asistir)

8. Almuerzo con Alonso y Lázaro. Siempre _____ con ellos. (quitarse, divertirse, ponerse)

9. Vuelvo a casa y _____ a hacer la tarea. (traer, poner, tener)

10. Ceno, leo y _____ a las once. ¡Necesito dormir! (levantarse, irse, acostarse)

B. **El día típico de Andrés.** Now that you've read Andrés's description of a typical day, describe it to someone else. Complete the following sentences with the present tense of the verb that best completes each sentence.

1. Cuando Andrés tiene clases, _____ (preocuparse, despertarse, llamarse) temprano.

2. No _____ en la cama. (quedarse, maquillarse, irse)

3. _____ en seguida. (acostarse, dormirse, levantarse)

4. _____ y se afeita. (ducharse, divertirse, quedarse)

5. Después, _____ la ropa y baja a la cocina para desayunar. (secarse, lavarse, ponerse)

6. A las ocho y diez, _____. (dormirse, irse, despertarse)

7. Llega a la universidad y _____ a sus clases. (tomar, escuchar, asistir)

8. Almuerza con Alonso y Lázaro. Siempre _____ con ellos. (quitarse, divertirse, ponerse)

9. Vuelve a casa y _____ a hacer la tarea. (traer, poner, tener)

10. Cena, lee y _____ a las once. ¡Necesita dormir! (levantarse, irse, acostarse)

La hora

A. **¿Qué hora es?** Write out the time shown on the clocks below.

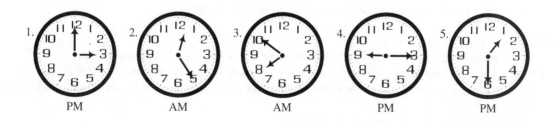

1. PM 2. AM 3. AM 4. PM 5. PM

1. _____

2. _____

3. _____

4. _____

5. _____

B. **¿A qué hora?** Look at this schedule of flight departures (**salidas**) from Bogotá to Buenos Aires and answer the questions that follow in complete sentences.

```
┌─────────────────────────────────────────┐
│               SALIDAS                     │
│                                           │
│      BOGOTÁ  ➜  BUENOS AIRES              │
│                                           │
│   Lunes a viernes    Sábado y domingo     │
│        6:00               6:45            │
│        9:15                               │
│       12:12              13:00            │
│       18:00              19:00            │
│       23:00                               │
└─────────────────────────────────────────┘
```

1. ¿Cuántos aviones salen los lunes de Bogotá para Buenos Aires?

   _____

2. ¿A qué hora sale el primer avión los jueves?

   _____

3. ¿A qué hora sale el último avión los martes?

   _____

4. ¿A qué hora sale el segundo avión los domingos?

   _____

5. ¿A qué hora sale el último avión los domingos?

   _____

Vamos a leer . . . .

A. Skim the following ad from a Chilean university and answer the questions.

1. What is the name of the university?
2. In which two Chilean cities is it located? (Hint: **la sede** means *headquarters* or *central office.*)
3. The ad is notifying prospective students that it is time to apply for the 1998 school year. (In most countries south of the Equator the academic year runs from March to December.) What would you guess is the term for "application"?
4. What kind of students is the university looking for?

Now read the ad more carefully and answer the following questions:

5. Which major can be studied in both cities?
6. Can you find the Spanish words for *law* and *journalism?*
7. One of the majors is in education. Which one?

8. What was the date of the admissions examination?
9. What preparation was necessary for the examination?

Vamos a explorar el ciberespacio . . . .

University Life. The World Wide Web offers many fascinating sites throughout the Spanish-speaking world dealing with the cultural topics in this lesson. Take a virtual field trip. Go to http://www.harcourtcollege.com/spanish/saludosrecuerdos to discover more.

Lección 5
La salud y el cuerpo

El cuerpo humano. . . . .

A. You've decided to go to medical school in Mexico. Will you pass this part of the entrance examination? Identify each part of the human body and write the word with the appropriate definite article on the line below.

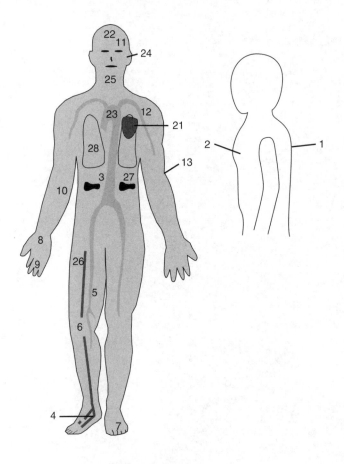

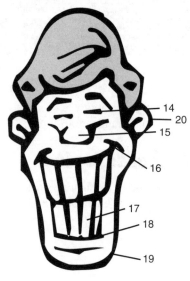

1. _____   15. _____

2. _____   16. _____

3. _____   17. _____

4. _____   18. _____

5. _____   19. _____

6. _____   20. _____

7. _____   21. _____

8. _____   22. _____

9. _____   23. _____

10. _____ 24. _____

11. _____ 25. _____

12. _____ 26. _____

13. _____ 27. _____

14. _____ 28. _____

B. Claudia is describing her symptoms to the doctor. Choose the correct completion for each of her sentences.

1. No puedo oír bien. Tengo dolor de...

    a. cabeza   **b.** oídos   **c.** brazos

2. No puedo escribir. Tengo problemas con...

    a. las rodillas   **b.** la nariz   **c.** la mano

3. No puedo correr. Tengo problemas con...

    a. los pies   **b.** las orejas   **c.** el cerebro

4. No puedo ver bien. Tengo problemas con...

    a. la espalda   **b.** el cuello   **c.** los ojos

5. No puedo hablar. Tengo dolor de...

    a. cerebro   **b.** manos   **c.** garganta

Otros verbos con cambio en el presente.................

A. Fill in the blanks below with the correct form of **pedir** in order to ask and answer the questions about what people are asking the doctor for.

1. ¿Qué _____ (tú), vitaminas o aspirinas? (Yo) _____

2. ¿Qué _____ (ella), una receta o una dieta? _____

3. ¿Qué _____ Uds., antibióticos o una inyección? _____

B. Complete with the appropriate form of **pedir** or **preguntar** according to the context.

1. El médico me _____ si tengo dolor.

2. Yo le _____ si necesito una receta.

3. Pienso _____ la medicina en la farmacia.

4. El empleado de la farmacia me _____ la receta.

5. Yo le _____ cuánto cuesta la medicina.

Expresiones con *tener*.................

A. Pick the appropriate **tener** expressions to complete the sentences below.

tener (mucho) frío, calor, miedo, sueño   tener que...
tener (mucha) sed, hambre, razón, prisa   tener ganas de...
tener...años

1. ¿Está lista la comida, mamá? Yo _____.

2. María sale corriendo de la casa. Creo que (ella) _____.

3. Sí, Juanito. Tegucigalpa es la capital de Honduras. (tú) _____.

4. Tienes que cerrar las ventanas. Los niños _____.

5. Abuela, queremos jugo. (nosotros) _____.

6. Hace noventa y cinco grados y no hay viento. Por eso (nosotros) _____.

7. El médico dice que yo necesito una operación. ¡Qué horror! (Yo) _____.

8. Yo _____ 19 años ahora. En junio cumplo *(turn)* veinte años.

9. No quiero pasar más tiempo en casa. _____ de salir. ¿Vienes?

10. ¿Por qué miras la tele, José? Mañana es tu examen. _____ estudiar.

El presente progresivo . . . .

A. ¡Gripe en la residencia! The flu is spreading through the dorm. What are these people doing at this moment to cure it or prevent it? Form sentences with the present progressive from the elements given.

> **MODELO• • • ➤** Luisa/tomar/mucha vitamina C
> **Luisa está tomando mucha vitamina C.**

1. Tomás y Pedro/llamar/al médico

_____

2. Paula y yo/prepararse/un té caliente

_____

3. Alfredo/dormir

_____

4. yo descansar

_____

5. tú/tomar/antibióticos

_____

Los pronombres de complemento directo. . . . .

A. Complete the following sentences with the correct present tense form of the verb in parentheses and the appropriate object pronoun.

> **MODELO• • • ➤** Marcos sabe la respuesta, pero (él) no _____ (decir).
> **Marcos sabe la respuesta, pero no la dice.**

1. Yo necesito vitaminas, y por eso (yo) _____ (pedir) en la farmacia.

2. Cuando los niños quieren jugo, la abuela siempre _____ (servir).

3. La puerta está abierta. Si tienes frío, (nosotros) _____ (cerrar).

4. No puedes lavar todos esos platos. Si quieres, yo _____ (ayudar).

5. ¿No _____ (recordar) Ud.? Soy Luis Alberto Soto Menéndez.

6. Vamos a hacer vegetales. Ahora (yo) _____ (cocinar).

B. Conversaciones. Create question and answer exchanges about health. Use the present tense and direct object pronouns. Write the answer to each question in two ways, as in the model.

> **MODELO• • • ➤** poder (tú)/hacer/los ejercicios/sí
> ¿Puedes hacer los ejercicios?
> **Sí, los puedo hacer.** _or_ **Sí, puedo hacerlos.**

1. tener que (Uds.)/seguir/la dieta/no

_____

_____

2. ir a (tú)/comer/muchos vegetales/sí

_____

_____

3. deber (yo)/evitar/el estrés/sí

_____

_____

4. poder (Ud.)/tomar/esta medicina/no

_____

_____

5. querer (tú)/ver/al médico/no

_____

_____

6. deber (nosotros)/pedir/la misma receta/sí

_____

_____

Vamos a leer. . . . .

A. **Clínicas de Guatemala.** Skim the following two ads for clinics found in the same issue of one of the main daily newspapers of Guatemala City, _Prensa Libre_.

1. What areas of health do these **clínicas** deal with? Use the illustrations and key words to help you figure it out. What key words do you find?

_____

2. What time of year did the second ad appear? What do you think the greeting **Feliz Navidad** means?

_____

3. Which **clínica** lists office hours? What do you think the word **consultas** means?

_____

4. Can you find the Spanish for the following phrases in the ads?

toothache _____

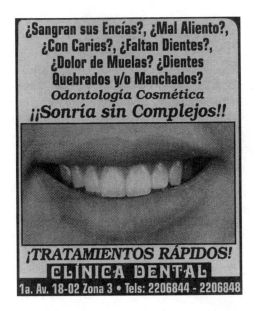

athlete's foot _____

treatment _____

cosmetic dentistry _____

5. Look at the following vocabulary list and answer the questions that follow.

el aliento	breath	**quebrado**	broken
las caries	tooth decay, cavities	**sangrar**	to bleed
el complejo	complex	**sin**	without
encarnado	lodged in the flesh	**sonreír**	to smile
la encía	gum (of the mouth)	**¡sonría!**	smile!
faltar	to be missing	**el sudor**	sweat
el hongo	fungus	**la uña**	fingernail, toenail
manchado	spotted	**la verruga**	wart
el olor	odor		

a. What gum problem does the dental clinic deal with?

_____

b. What problems of the teeth are treated there?

_____

c. What condition is designated by **uñas encarnadas?**

_____

d. What odor problems are handled at the clinics?

_____

e. What does **¡¡Sonría sin complejos!!** mean?

_____

B. La vida de un joven médico. Read the following narrative by a young doctor and answer the questions that follow.

Yo me llamo Eduardo Mendoza. Soy médico. Trabajo en un consultorio *(doctor's office)* con varios otros médicos en una ciudad de la montaña. Estos días estoy muy ocupado. Estamos viendo muchos casos *(cases)* de gripe. Cuando los enfermos llegan al consultorio para vernos, están tosiendo y estornudando. Muchos tienen dolor de cabeza y están roncos. Algunos están tan enfermos que tienen problemas con los pulmones y tienen que ir al hospital. Otros dicen que tienen dolor de espalda. Les *(to/for them)* receto medicinas para la tos y les recomiendo aspirinas para el dolor. Los otros médicos y yo estamos trabajando hasta las nueve de la noche todos los días. Estamos muy cansados, pero nuestros pacientes nos necesitan.

1. Eduardo Mendoza...
   a. trabaja con otros médicos.
   b. tiene gripe.
   c. va a ver al médico.

2. Está muy ocupado porque...
   a. tiene un consultorio nuevo.
   b. el consultorio está muy lejos de su casa.
   c. tiene muchos pacientes con gripe.

3. Los enfermos que tienen gripe...
   a. tienen problemas con las rodillas.
   b. tosen y estornudan.
   c. no quieren ver al médico.

4. El doctor Mendoza receta aspirinas...
   a. para el dolor de cabeza.
   b. para los problemas de los pulmones.
   c. para los médicos ocupados.

5. Hay tantos enfermos que los médicos...
   a. no quieren trabajar.
   b. tienen que trabajar hasta tarde.
   c. están roncos.

Vamos a explorar el ciberespacio . . . .

The Five Senses. The World Wide Web offers many fascinating sites throughout the Spanish-speaking world dealing with the cultural topics in this lesson. Take a virtual field trip. Go to http://www.harcourtcollege.com/spanish/saludosrecuerdos to discover more.

Lección 6
En la tienda de ropa

La ropa ....

A. **¿Cómo es esta ropa?** Describe each item of clothing in a sentence that includes the color and material given. Follow the model.

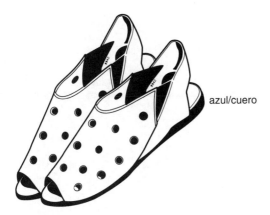

azul/cuero

MODELO•••➤ ➜ Las sandalias azules son de cuero.

negro/lana

1. _____

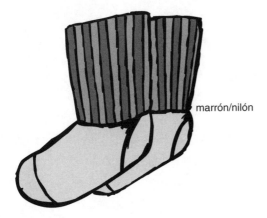

marrón/nilón

2. _____

amarillo/seda

3. _____

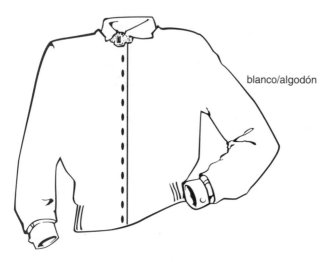

blanco/algodón

4. _____

gris/poliéster

5. _____

B. **¿Qué ropa ponerse?** Look at each drawing and write a sentence or two listing what you would wear for the weather or occasion depicted. When appropriate, mention the material that the clothing is made of. You can choose from the list below and add any other items you choose.

blusa/falda/vestido/medias/calcetines/pantalones/traje/chaqueta/abrigo/sudadera/traje de baño/camiseta/cinturón/impermeable/botas/pantalón corto/vaqueros *(jeans)*/sombrero/gorra/camisa/de seda/de algodón/de lana/de poliéster

MODELO ● ● ● ➤   Cuando hace calor me pongo una camisa de algodón y un pantalón corto.

1. _____

_____

_____

2. _____

_____

_____

3. _____

_____

_____

4. _____

_____

_____

5. _____

_____

_____

Los adjetivos y pronombres demostrativos . . . .

A. **¡Tantos hijos!** Mrs. Olivera is trying to help her six children get dressed this morning. She suggests clothing to them, but each one picks something else to wear. Write the children's answers to their mother's questions using the demonstrative adjectives and pronouns as in the model.

MODELO• • • ➤ Luisa, ¿vas a ponerte esta blusa?
¿Esa blusa? No, mamá. Quiero ponerme aquélla.

1. Luisa, ¿vas a ponerte estos zapatos?

_____

2. Javier, ¿vas a ponerte estos pantalones?

_____

3. Margarita, ¿vas a ponerte este vestido?

_____

4. Gabriel, ¿vas a ponerte esta camisa?

_____

5. Lidia, ¿vas a ponerte estas botas?

_____

6. Marcos, ¿vas a ponerte esta sudadera?

_____

B. **En la tienda de ropa.** Carolina is shopping at a clothing boutique. The salesclerk suggests various things to her, but in each case Carolina decides on something else. Write Carolina's responses to the salesclerk's suggestions using the demonstrative adjectives and pronouns as in the model.

MODELO • • ➤   Este cinturón es muy bonito, señorita.
                             No, ése no me gusta. Aquel cinturón me gusta más.

1. Esta falda es muy bonita, señorita.

_____

2. Este paraguas es muy bonito, señorita.

_____

3. Estas cadenas de oro son muy bonitas, señorita.

_____

4. Estos aretes son muy bonitos, señorita.

_____

5. Este suéter es muy bonito, señorita.

_____

6. Estas sandalias son muy bonitas, señorita.

_____

El imperfecto del pasado . . . .

A. **Recuerdos.** Silvia is remembering her aunt Rosaura. Complete her narration by filling in the imperfect of the verbs in parentheses.

Yo recuerdo mucho a mi tía Rosaura. Ella _____ (1. ser) una mujer muy elegante.

_____ (2. comprar) ropa de calidad y _____ (3. saber) vestirse. _____

(4. llevar) trajes a la moda y siempre _____ (5. usar) zapatos de tacón. Cuando _____

(6. salir) a la calle, _____ (7. ponerse) un sombrero y _____ (8. llevar) un bolso de

cuero. Nosotras la _____ (9. admirar) mucho y _____ (10. querer) ser como ella.

B. **Cuando yo era niño(a)...** Tell about your life as a child by answering the following questions in complete sentences.

1. ¿Dónde vivía Ud. de niño(a)?

_____

_____

2. ¿Qué ropa llevaba para ir a la escuela?

_____

_____

3. ¿Escogía Ud. su propia ropa o le compraba la ropa su mamá?

_____

_____

4. ¿Le gustaba la escuela de niño(a)?

_____

_____

5. ¿Tenía muchos amigos? ¿Quién era su mejor amigo(a)?

_____

_____

6. ¿A qué jugaba con sus amigos?

_____

_____

Los pronombres de complemento indirecto . . . .

A. **¿A quién?** Answer each of the following questions affirmatively, using the indirect object in parentheses. Add the correct indirect object pronoun.

MODELO● ● ● ➤ ¿La tienda devolvió el dinero? (a los clientes)
Sí, la tienda les devolvió el dinero a los clientes.

1. ¿Mandaste las invitaciones? (a todos mis amigos)

_____

2. ¿Regalaste la pulsera? (a mi novia)

_____

3. ¿Juan prestó sus casetes? (a mí)

_____

4. ¿Escribieron Uds. la carta? (a Carlos Pérez)

_____

5. ¿El profesor dijo las respuestas? (a los estudiantes)

_____

6. ¿Compraron Uds. un regalo? (a ti)

_____

B. Hay que ayudar a la gente. Your friend asks if people need certain things. You suggest that you and your friend help them out using the verb in parentheses and the appropriate indirect object pronoun.

MODELO•• • ➤ ¿Carlos necesita aquel libro? (dar)
Sí. ¿Por qué no le damos aquel libro a Carlos?

1. ¿Los chicos necesitan estas corbatas? (prestar)

_____

2. ¿Marcos necesita su paraguas? (devolver)

_____

3. ¿Carolina necesita una sudadera roja? (regalar)

_____

4. ¿Pablito necesita una gorra de lana? (comprar)

_____

5. ¿Matilde y Julia necesitan saber la dirección de la tienda? (decir)

_____

6. ¿Sergio y Andrés necesitan ver el catálogo? (enseñar)

_____

Los pronombres indirectos con _gustar_ y verbos similares . . .

A. Opiniones y reacciones. Write what people think and feel by using **gustar** and verbs like it to answer the following questions. Use the verbs and the information given to construct your answers.

MODELO•• • ➤ ¿Qué dices de la fiesta? (gustar: la comida—sí, las decoraciones—no)
Me gusta la comida, pero no me gustan las decoraciones.

1. ¿Qué piensas de este viaje? (gustar: los hoteles—sí, la comida—no)

_____

2. ¿Qué piensa Julián del colegio? (interesar: la historia—sí, las ciencias—no)

_____

3. ¿Qué te pasa? (doler: los oídos—sí, la garganta—no)

_____

4. ¿Qué deportes prefieren Uds.? (encantar: el fútbol—sí, la natación—no)

_____

5. ¿Qué te parece esta ropa? (parecer: las blusas—lindas, el vestido—feo)

_____

6. ¿Qué prefieren hacer Marta y Luis cuando no trabajan? (gustar: el teatro—sí, los partidos—no)

_____

B. **La moda de hoy.** Talk about what you like and dislike in today's fashions. What kind of clothing and material do you like best? What do your friends like? Write a paragraph about tastes in clothing using verbs such as **gustar, interesar, encantar, parecer bien/mal/caro,** etc.

_____

_____

_____

_____

_____

_____

_____

_____

_____

_____

_____

_____

Vamos a leer . . . .

This ad for El Corte Inglés, Spain's most famous department store, appeared recently in the Madrid newspaper *ABC.* Skim the ad quickly and answer the following questions.

1. What is the ad asking people to celebrate?

_____

2. Until when is the sale on?

_____

3. What word is used to emphasize the huge mark-downs offered?

_____

4. How do the hours of El Corte Inglés differ from store hours in the United States?

_____

Para celebrar el fin de año,
El Corte Inglés ha seleccionado
para usted 98 felices artículos,
con una calidad y un precio
que son un auténtico regalo.
Hasta el 31 de diciembre.

¡CELÉBRELO CON NOSOTROS!

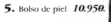

1. Chaquetón de novak **30%** de descuento. **2.** Twin-set de punto **4.995.** **3.** Pantalón de pata

de gallo **4.985.** **4.** Colgante de metal plateado y cristal **2.475.** **5.** Bolso de piel **10.950.** **6.** Camisa

de vestir y sport para hombre: una **3.750** dos **7.000.** **7.** Corbata de seda natural **2.250.** **8.** Zapatos de piel para

hombre **6.950.** **9.** Jersey de cuello redondo Dustin **3.500.** **10.** Polares para chicos **3.995.**

11. Para chicas. Chaqueta **11.900** Pantalón **5.900.** **12.** Chaquetón para niña, tallas 4-16 **7.995.** **13.** Buzo para

bebés, hasta 1 año **4.995.** **14.** Balón de fútbol Nike **6.950.** **15.** Botas de baloncesto Reebok Shaq Steel

9.950. **16.** Juego para PC FIFA 98 **4.995.** **17.** Vídeos: trilogía de Brad Pitt **2.995.**

18. Aspirador Solac **10.995.** **19.** Manta de viaje **3.795.** **20.** Lámpara portátil con pantalla, pie de

madera **2.400. 21.** Cava extra Codorniu, botella de 75 cl. **669. 22.** Uvas de la suerte **495** PTA/kg.

…Y así, hasta 98 felices artículos.

El Corte Inglés

y Tiendas *El Corte Inglés* *
ESPECIALISTAS EN TI.

* Sólo en Tiendas donde existe exposición de esta mercancía

MAÑANA DOMINGO ABRIMOS DE 11 A 21 H. MADRID
LA VAGUADA, PARQUESUR Y TIENDAS EL CORTE INGLÉS DE 10 A 22 H.

5. En los países hispanos, se dan regalos tradicionalmente para el día de Los Reyes Magos, el 6 de enero, y a veces también para Navidad. Estudie el anuncio y conteste estas preguntas:

a. ¿Qué le va Ud. a regalar a su mejor amigo(a)?

_____

b. ¿Qué le va Ud. a regalar a su mamá o a su papá?

_____

c. ¿Qué le va Ud. a comprar a su hermano(a) o a su sobrino(a)?

_____

d. Y ¿qué le van a regalar a Ud.?

_____

Vamos a explorar el ciberespacio . . . .

Clothing. The World Wide Web offers many fascinating sites throughout the Spanish-speaking world dealing with the cultural topics in this lesson. Take a virtual field trip. Go to http://www.harcourtcollege.com/spanish/ saludosrecuerdos to discover more.

Lección 7

El hogar y los muebles

El hogar y los muebles . . . .

A. Indicate whether each of these statments about the Vallejo house is **C** *(cierto)* or **F** *(falso)*.

1. La casa tiene cuatro dormitorios.	C	F
2. La cocina no es muy moderna.	C	F
3. Hay lugar para dos coches en el garaje.	C	F
4. Hay un refrigerador en el comedor.	C	F
5. Hay mesitas al lado del sofá.	C	F
6. Hay seis sillas en el comedor.	C	F
7. Hay cuatro sillones en la sala.	C	F
8. Hay un sofá en el dormitorio.	C	F
9. El televisor está en el comedor.	C	F
10. Todas las habitaciones tienen ventana.	C	F

El pretérito de los verbos en *-ar* . . . .

A. Find out how Zoila found a new apartment by completing her story with the preterit of the verbs in parentheses.

El lunes por fin yo _____ (1. alquilar—*to rent*) un apartamento. _____ (2. Empezar) a buscar la semana pasada. Ese día _____ (3. levantarse) temprano, _____ (4. comprar) el periódico, y _____ (5. mirar) los anuncios. Por la mañana _____ (6. buscar), pero no _____ (7. encontrar) nada. _____ (8. Hablar) con una amiga. Ella me _____ (9. recomendar) una agencia. _____ (10. Llamar) a la agencia y ellos me _____ (11. enseñar) varios apartamentos. Uno de los apartamentos me _____ (12. gustar) mucho. (yo) _____ (13. Mudarse) al día siguiente. Mis amigos me _____ (14. ayudar) y yo los _____ (15. invitar) a comer. Nosotros _____ (16. trabajar) mucho, pero lo _____ (17. pasar) bien, y ¡ _____ (18. terminar) la mudanza en un solo día!

El pretérito de los verbos en *-er* y *-ir* . . . .

A. **Fue ayer.** Answer each of the following questions saying that the action asked about happened yesterday.

MODELO• • • ➤ ¿Juan le escribe a Ud.?
Sí, me escribió ayer.

1. ¿Come Ud. tacos?

_____

2. ¿Recibe Ud. correo electrónico?

_____

3. ¿Corre Ud.?

_____

4. ¿Oye Ud. música?

_____

5. ¿Sale Ud. con los amigos?

_____

6. ¿Lee Ud. el periódico?

_____

7. ¿Asiste Ud. al concierto?

_____

8. ¿Va Ud. a la biblioteca?

_____

B. **Entre amigos.** Tell what this group of friends did yesterday by creating sentences out of each string of elements. Write your sentences in the preterit.

MODELO• • • ➤   Juan/quedarse en casa
                       Juan se quedó en casa.

1. Marta/ir a la universidad

_____

2. José/dormir toda la mañana

_____

3. Sara y Marcos/repetir el nuevo vocabulario

_____

4. Luis/pedirle ayuda al profesor de química

_____

5. La cafetería/servir comida mexicana

_____

6. Los estudiantes/divertirse comiendo tacos y enchiladas

_____

7. Carolina/preferir comer en casa

_____

8. Ella/no divertirse

_____

9. Lola/leer cien páginas

_____

10. Yo/leer doscientas páginas

_____

La combinación de dos complementos ....

A. **Mala memoria.** You remind your friend Carlos to do several things. In each case Carlos tells you he did it. Write Carlos's answers to you using double object pronouns.

MODELO• • • ➤   Ud.: ¿Cuándo me das el sillón viejo?
                       Carlos: ¿No te acuerdas? Ya te lo di.

1. ¿Cuándo me enseñas tu piscina?

   _____

2. ¿Cuándo me devuelves el microondas?

   _____

3. ¿Cuándo me regalas la alfombra vieja?

   _____

4. ¿Cuándo me das las lámparas?

   _____

5. ¿Cuándo me vendes los muebles?

   _____

6. ¿Cuándo me alquilas el garaje para mi coche?

   _____

B. Ya lo hicimos. Some work-study students tell their advisor that they have already done the things he asks about. Use double object pronouns and the verb in parentheses to write their answers to the advisor.

   MODELO● ● ● ➤   El nuevo profesor quiere ver el comedor de la universidad. (enseñar)
   Ya se lo enseñamos.

1. Josefina Díaz necesita los libros de química. (dar)

   _____

2. La profesora Martínez quiere un sillón para su sala de clase. (buscar)

   _____

3. Mi secretaria ya no quiere los muebles que tiene en la oficina. (sacar)

   _____

4. El profesor Páez dijo que las ventanas de su sala de clase estaban sucias. (limpiar)

   _____

5. Los profesores tienen que entregar las notas. (pedir)

   _____

6. En la reunión de profesores pidieron café. (servir)

   _____

Los números 100–1000+ . . . .

A. **Comprando muebles.** Complete each of the following checks that people have written to purchase the furniture and appliances shown. Write out the price and write the item shown on the memo line.

MODELO• • • ➤

Banco de Miami	
	$ 355.00
	5 de marzo del 2001
Páguese a la orden de Mueblerías Hernández	
la suma de trescientos cincuenta y cinco dólares	
Por estéreo	*Rogelio Rodríguez*

1.

Banco de Miami	
	$ 590.00
	2 de febrero del 2001
Páguese a la orden de Alfredo Villamos	
la suma de _____	
Por _____	*Catalina Márquez Soto*

2.

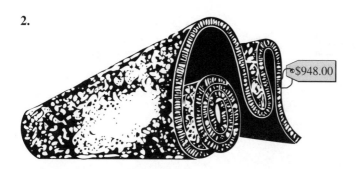

$948.00

Banco de Miami	
	$ __948.00__
	__17 de octubre__ del __2001__

Páguese a la orden de ___Almacenes Farinelli___

la suma de _____

Por _____   _Enrique Chamaco Zapata_

3.

$102.00

Banco de Miami	
	$ __102.00__
	__5 de junio__ del __2001__

Páguese a la orden de ___Tomás de Mónica___

la suma de _____

Por _____   _Ana María Ibáñez de Zúñiga_

4.

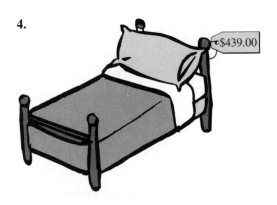

$439.00

Banco de Miami	
	$ __439.00__
	__30 de noviembre__ del __2001__

Páguese a la orden de ___El Dormitorio Moderno___

la suma de _____

Por _____ ___Juan Alberto Salas Sotomayor___

5.

$789.00

Banco de Miami	
	$ __789.00__
	__25 de mayo__ del __2001__

Páguese a la orden de ___Electrodomésticos Venezuela___

la suma de _____

Por _____ ___Margarita Pérez Molina___

Vamos a leer . . . .

A. Read these two ads from the classifieds of *El Universal*, one of the major daily newspapers of Caracas, Venezuela. As you scan them, can you tell what kind of residences each one offers?

> **PRADOS DEL ESTE, AV. EL PASEO, QUIN-**
> ta María Pía, vendo magnífica quinta, 230 millo-
> nes. También alquilo 3.000 dólares mensuales,
> 500 metros construcción, 1.200 metros terreno
> con árboles frutales. Puede visitarse cualquier
> hora. Telfs. 616933, 613407.
> **REVALORICE SU PROPIEDAD, INCREMEN-**
> te el valor de su inmueble. Asesoría profesional
> a su alcance. Consulte con Artespacio, teléfono:
> 2650080, 014.9374243.
> **URBANIZACIÓN LOS NARANJOS, VENDO**
> fabulosa quinta tres niveles, espectacular pano-
> rámica, salones múltiples usoss, terraza, jardi-
> nes, cuatro habitaciones, estudio, biblioteca, bar,
> todas comodidades. Teléfonos: 02.9860003,
> 014.9057403.

> **LA UNIÓN, TOWN HOUSE 189 MTS. +60**
> terraza, 3 hab. +2 baños, Hs/B. salón, come-
> dor, 2 ptos. estac., vigilancia, 10.000.000 mts.
> de áreas verdes, Ernesto Sosa & Asociados.
> 261.0915/ 0360, 266.2886, (014)923.2621.

1. What word is used for *terrace* in the ads?

_____

2. What do the following abbreviations mean?

hab. _____

mts. _____

3. What word is used for *large private house* in Venezuela?

_____

4. How many levels does the house in Los Naranjos have? What is the Spanish word for *level?*

_____

5. Which of the two residences offers more space?

_____

6. One of the residences has on-site security. What word tells you this?

_____

7. How many bedrooms does each residence have?

_____

8. What is appealing about the setting of La Unión Town House?

_____

Vamos a explorar el ciberespacio . . . .

Housing. The World Wide Web offers many fascinating sites throughout the Spanish-speaking world dealing with the cultural topics in this lesson. Take a virtual field trip. Go to http://www.harcourtcollege.com/spanish/saludos recuerdos to discover more.

Lección 8

De viaje

En el aeropuerto. . . . .

A. Look at the following drawing of an airport and identify each of the following words by writing the letter of the person or object it corresponds to in the picture.

1. _____ la aduana

2. _____ la tarjeta de embarque

3. _____ el avión

4. _____ la puerta

5. _____ el equipaje

6. _____ el asiento

7. _____ la ventanilla

8. _____ los pasajeros

9. _____ el boleto

10. _____ la agenta

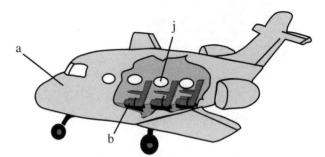

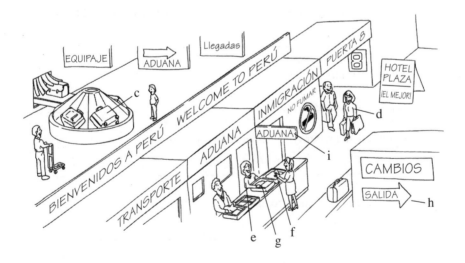

B. La señora Arias hizo un viaje (took a trip). Tell the story of Mrs. Arias's trip by putting these events in logical order. Number them 1–8.

_____ saludó al agente

_____ llegó al aeropuerto

_____ recibió su tarjeta de embarque

_____ tuvo que hacer cola

_____ fue al aeropuerto en taxi

_____ se acercó a mostrador

_____ enseñó su boleto

_____ fue a la puerta para abordar

C. ¿Temprano o tarde? Read the following conversation between Lucas and the airline clerk about a mix-up. Then complete a summary of the conversation by adding the missing words.

Lucas: Señorita, por favor, ¿por cuál puerta sale el vuelo trescientos ochenta y cinco para Lima?
Agente: ¿El vuelo trescientos ochenta y cinco? Salió hace quince minutos. *(It left fifteen minutes ago.)*
Lucas: ¿Qué dice usted? ¿Que salió? Pero esto es la cosa más grande. ¡Ahora los vuelos salen antes de tiempo y dejan a los pasajeros en el aeropuerto!
Agente: Usted está equivocado, señor. El vuelo salió puntual a las ocho y veinte.
Lucas: Tiene que haber *(There has to be)* algún error. Yo creo que en este aeropuerto todos trabajen sin poner atención a la hora.
Agente: Mire Ud., señor. El avión no salió antes de tiempo. Usted llegó tarde. Por eso perdió el avión.
Lucas: Pero yo estaba aquí en el restaurante tomando café. Miré mi reloj que decía que eran las ocho menos diez. Leía mi novela y no escuchaba los avisos.
Agente: ¿Y qué dice su reloj ahora?
Lucas: Las ocho menos diez... ¡Las ocho menos diez! ¡Dios mío, mi reloj no anda!
Agente: Pero los relojes nuestros sí andan.
Lucas: ¡Qué tontería! Mire, señorita. Tengo que estar en Lima hoy por la tarde. ¿A qué hora es el próximo vuelo?
Agente: A las diez y media, pero creo que está completo. Voy a ver lo que dice la computadora... Bueno, usted tiene suerte. Queda un solo asiento.
Lucas: Bueno, cámbieme el pasaje. No quiero más problemas.
Agente: En ese caso, debe comprarse otro reloj.

Cuando Lucas llegó al aeropuerto, preguntó por cuál (1) _____ salía su avión. La agente le

dijo: "Salió hace (2) _____ minutos." Lucas creyó que el avión salió (3) _____.

Le dijo a la agente que la gente que trabajaba en el aeropuerto no ponía (4) _____ a la hora.

La agente le explicó a Lucas que el vuelo salió (5) _____, pero que él llegó

(6) _____. Lucas perdió el avión porque su (7) _____ no andaba. Él estaba en el

(8) _____ tomando café y leyendo su (9) _____ y no escuchaba los avisos. Había

otro (10) _____ para Lima a las diez y media y la agente dijo que había un solo

(11) _____. Ella le cambió el pasaje a Lucas y le dijo que lo que necesitaba era

(12) _____ reloj.

El pretérito de los verbos irregulares..................

A. Escoja la forma del verbo que mejor complete la frase y escríbala en el espacio.

1. Los Molina (hizo, hicieron, fuiste) _____ un viaje por Sudamérica.

2. Yo (fue, hice, fui) _____ con ellos.

3. (Hizo, Fue, Estuvo) _____ muy buen tiempo.

4. (Hiciste, Estuvo, Fuimos) _____ a cinco países.

5. Pero no (tuvimos, estuvimos, pudimos) _____ ir a Chile. ¡Qué pena!

B. Escriba el pretérito del verbo que mejor complete la frase.

1. Ayer yo (divertirse, despertarse, enojarse) _____ temprano.

2. Pero no (poder, tener, saber) _____ levantarme porque me sentía mal.

3. Tenía pasaje de avión para Puerto Rico, pero (traer, hacer, tener) _____ que llamar al aeropuerto para confirmar.

4. Yo le (estar, decir, venir) _____ a la agente que tenía que cambiar mi pasaje.

5. Ella me (dar, tener, hacer) _____ un asiento en el vuelo del viernes.

6. Mi amigo Juan me (venir, tener, traer) _____ el periódico.

7. Yo (quedarse, levantarse, afeitarse) _____ todo el día en cama.

8. Al día siguiente (acostarse, sentirse, lavarse) _____ mejor.

9. Y el viernes (ir, estar, hacer) _____ a Puerto Rico.

C. Ya lo hicieron. Answer each of the following questions saying that the people asked about already did these things. Use the preterit in your responses. Replace object nouns by the corresponding pronouns.

MODELO• • • ➤ ¿Ellos van a salir?
Ya salieron.

1. ¿Te van a decir la hora del vuelo?

_____

2. ¿Vas a poner tu maletín debajo de tu asiento?

_____

3. ¿El empleado nos va a dar los comprobantes?

_____

4. ¿Juan va a hacer la maleta?

_____

5. ¿Va a venir el avión?

_____

6. ¿Rosalba va a hacer un viaje?

_____

Contrastes entre el imperfecto y el pretérito . . . .

A. **¿Imperfecto o pretérito?** Rehaga esta narración en el pasado. Decida entre el imperfecto y el pretérito según el contexto.

1. Diego Sánchez _nace_ en Santiago de Chile.

2. _Es_ un niño inteligente y sociable.

3. Siempre le _gustan_ los aviones.

4. En el colegio _es_ un buen estudiante.

5. Pero _no quiere (refuses)_ ir a la universidad.

6. _Se hace (He becomes)_ piloto.

7. _Consigue_ un puesto _(He gets a job)_ con LAN-Chile, la línea nacional.

8. En uno de sus viajes a México, _conoce_ a Lidia Arredón.

9. Los padres de ella _tienen_ hoteles en Acapulco.

10. Diego y Lidia _se enamoran_ y _se casan._

11. A los cuarenta años, Diego _decide_ que no _quiere_ volar más.

12. Él y Lidia _empiezan_ a trabajar en los hoteles.

B. **Una carta.** Marcela Ibáñez is traveling to Europe where she will spend a year abroad studying. Complete the letter she wrote to her parents to tell them about the trip to Europe. Select either the imperfect or the preterit in each case.

Queridos padres:

¡El viaje (1. ser) _____ fantástico! El avión (2. salir) _____ y (3. llegar)

_____ puntualmente. Los asientos (4. ser) _____ cómodos y (5. haber)

_____ muchos estudiantes en el vuelo. Yo (6. conocer) _____ a mucha gente sim-

pática. En el avión los asistentes de vuelo _(flight attendants)_ nos (7. servir) _____ una comida

muy rica. Para pasar el tiempo, los otros estudiantes y yo (8. conversar) _____. Algunos (9. leer)

_____, otros (10. jugar) _____ ajedrez (*chess*). Después de la comida,

(11. ellos/pasar) _____ una película (*film*). Yo (12. decidir) _____ no verla porque

(13. querer) _____ hablar con mis nuevos amigos. En la última parte del vuelo, mucha gente se

(14. dormir) _____. Aunque yo (15. estar) _____ cansada, no (16. poder) (*I failed to*)

_____ dormirme, y (17. pasar) _____ las últimas horas del vuelo pensando en

Europa.

El avión (18. aterrizar—*land*) _____ en Barajas (*Madrid airport*) a las siete y media de la

mañana. Todos (19. nosotros/bajar) _____ del avión y (20. ir) _____ a buscar nuestro

equipaje. Yo (21. pasar) _____ a la aduana, los aduaneros me (22. hacer) _____ unas

preguntas, y (23. yo/buscar) _____ un taxi. Cuando (24. yo/llegar) _____ al hotel,

(25. ser) _____ las nueve y media. (26. Yo/querer) (*I wanted to*) _____ salir a ver la

ciudad, pero (27. yo/estar) _____ tan cansada que no (28. yo/poder) _____.

(29. Yo/acostarse) _____ y (30. dormir) _____ unas horas.

Mañana les escribo más. Muchos besos (*kisses*) y abrazos (*hugs*) de su hija.

C. Write a ten-sentence description of a trip you took. Write it in the past, choosing between the imperfect and the preterit for each verb. You will find these expressions useful:

with the imperfect: **poco a poco, generalmente, como de costumbre, mientras**
with the preterit: **de pronto, en seguida (inmediatamente), el día anterior**

_____

_____

_____

_____

_____

_____

_____

_____

_____

_____

_____

Las comparaciones de desigualdad............................

A. **Write two sentences to describe each situation.** Follow the model.

MODELO• • • ➤ el autobús/ser/más/barato/el tren : menos/cómodo
    El autobús es más barato que el tren. Es menos cómodo que el tren.

1. el viaje a Buenos Aires/ser/más/largo/el viaje a París : menos/fácil

_____

_____

2. Brasil/más/grande/Honduras : más/caro

_____

_____

3. en Panamá/hace/más/calor/en Chile : hace/menos/fresco

_____

_____

4. la comida vegetariana/ser/más/sabrosa/esta comida : ser/mejor

_____

_____

5. el avión/ser/más/rápido/el tren : ser/mejor

_____

_____

6. esta ciudad/ser/más/ruidosa/la capital : ser/peor

_____

_____

Las comparaciones de igualdad............................

A. **Gente afín _(well-matched people)_.** The people in this group of friends are very much alike. Say so using comparisons of equality. Remember that adjectives agree with the nouns they modify in gender and number.

MODELO• • • ➤ Ana/simpático/Alfredo
    Ana es tan simpática como Alfredo.

1. Margarita/generoso/Isabel

_____

2. Samuel/inteligente/Marisa

_____

3. Carolina/buena/Bárbara

_____

4. Amalia/estudioso/Pedro

_____

5. Víctor/amante de los deportes/Manuel

_____

B. **Muchos viajes.** Indicate that your friend has as many things for traveling as you do.

MODELO● ● ● ➤   boletos   **tantos boletos como yo**

1. comprobantes _____

2. tarjetas de embarque _____

3. maletas _____

4. pasajes _____

5. equipaje _____

6. vuelos _____

Vamos a leer. . . . .

A. This travel ad appeared recently in the Madrid newspaper _ABC_. Skim the ad quickly and answer the following questions.

1. What is the ad offering?

_____

2. Identify the points of departure and the destination.

_____

3. What are the numbers 48.900 and 106.800?

_____

Now read the ad carefully and answer these questions.

4. ¿Cuántas veces por semana sale el avión?

_____

5. ¿Qué recibe el cliente por 106.800 pesetas, además del avión?

_____

6. ¿Qué pasa si uno sale de Barcelona o Palma de Mallorca?

_____

7. ¿Es grande la compañía Marsans? Explique su respuesta.

_____

8. ¿Por qué es mejor comprar los pasajes sin esperar?

_____

Vamos a explorar el ciberespacio . . . .

Travel by Air. The World Wide Web offers many fascinating sites throughout the Spanish-speaking world dealing with the cultural topics in this lesson. Take a virtual field trip. Go to http://www.harcourtcollege.com/spanish/ saludosrecuerdos to discover more.

Lección 9
En el hotel

A. Look at the following drawing of a hotel room and identify each of the following words by writing the letter of the person or object it corresponds to in the picture.

1. _____ la bombilla

2. _____ la camarera

3. _____ la ventana

4. _____ el aire acondicionado

5. _____ el inodoro

6. _____ las toallas

7. _____ la cama

8. _____ la lámpara

9. _____ el ropero

10. _____ el teléfono

11. _____ el espejo

12. _____ la ducha

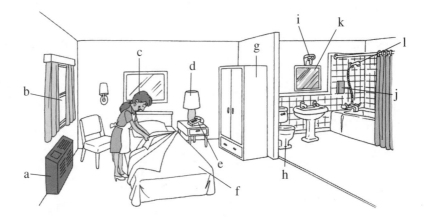

A. Here is an ad for a hotel in Mexico. Skim the ad quickly and answer the following questions.

¡Disfrute Oaxaca estas vacaciones con el paquete VICTORIA!

A sólo 4 1/2 hrs. de la Ciudad de México se impone el Hotel Victoria, con una espectacular vista panorámica, hermosos jardines, cancha de tenis etc., rodeado de cultura, tradición y mucha diversión

Incluye:
• Habitación doble en Estándar, Villa o Junior Suite.
• 2 niños gratis menores de 14 años en Villas o Junior Suite.
• Desayuno Americano o Buffet para dos adultos y dos niños.
• 15% de descuento en comidas y cenas.

• Usted obtiene un abono de $75.00 para alimentos y bebidas al presentar los comprobantes de las casetas.
• Coctel de bienvenida.
• 15% de descuento en tours con la agencia del hotel.

Precio por habitación por noche :	
Estándar	$550.00
Villa	$650.00
Junior Suite	$750.00

* Estancia mínima 2 noches
* Persona extra $80.00 incluye desayuno sólo en Villas y Junior Suite
* No incluye impuestos ni propinas

Reservaciones México:
280-18-70
Fax: 280-04-98

Oaxaca:
(951) 526-33
Fax: 524-11

HOTEL VICTORIA ★★★★★ OAXACA

Promoción válida del 01 de febrero al 13 de julio y del 15 de agosto al 26 de octubre de 1998. *No válido en Semana Santa*
Comisionable a agencia al 15%. Sujeto a espacio.

1. ¿Cuál es el nombre del hotel?

2. ¿En qué ciudad se encuentra?

3. ¿Cuántos tipos de habitación tiene?

Now read the ad carefully and answer these questions.

4. ¿A cuánta distancia queda este hotel de la capital de México?

5. ¿Qué deporte se puede practicar en el hotel?

6. ¿Qué incluye el precio de la habitación? ¿Qué no incluye?

7. ¿Qué descuentos se ofrecen a los huéspedes?

8. ¿Esta oferta es válida si el viajero se queda una sola noche?

Los mandatos formales ·

A. Consejos para el viaje. Mrs. Olivera is telling her friend Mrs. González what to do to get ready for her trip to Venezuela. Write out what she tells her as formal **Ud.** commands.

> **MODELO** • • • ➤ llamar al agente de viajes
> **Llame al agente de viajes.**

1. reservar una habitación

_____

2. preguntar si hay aire acondicionado

_____

3. hacer las maletas

_____

4. leer una guía turística

_____

5. no llevar muchas cosas

_____

6. pagar con tarjeta de crédito

_____

7. dejar su casa cerrada

_____

8. llegar al aeropuerto dos horas antes del vuelo

_____

B. Ya nos vamos. Mr. Laínez is leaving on a trip with his sixteen-year-old twins. He tells them what to do to get ready to go. Write what he says to the twins using **Uds.** commands.

> **MODELO** • • • ➤ cerrar las maletas
> **Cierren las maletas.**

1. poner los boletos en el bolsillo de mi impermeable

_____

2. apagar la luz

_____

3. no dejar el radio encendido

_____

4. pedir un taxi

_____

5. traer las maletas a la puerta

_____

6. buscar el correo de hoy

_____

7. sacar la basura

_____

8. no discutir más

_____

C. **Hablando con el botones.** Mr. and Mrs. Domínguez have just arrived at a hotel in Mexico. The bellhop is asking them questions. They answer him in each case with an affirmative **Ud.** command, replacing the direct object noun of his question with an object pronoun.

MODELO • • ➤ ¿Debo poner las maletas aquí?
      Sí, póngalas aquí.

1. ¿Debo colgar _(to hang up)_ los abrigos?

_____

2. ¿Debo cerrar las ventanas?

_____

3. ¿Debo poner el aire acondicionado?

_____

4. ¿Debo apagar la luz del baño?

_____

5. ¿Debo traer más toallas?

_____

6. ¿Debo llamar a la camarera?

_____

7. ¿Debo buscar un plano de la ciudad?

_____

D. Contradicciones. Juanito and Lidia Ponce ask their parents what they should do. Their mother answers with commands telling them to do what they ask, and their father tells them not to do these things. Replace any direct object nouns by pronouns. Write what Mrs. and Mr. Ponce say.

MODELO• • • ➤ ¿Nos levantamos a las seis?
  Señora Ponce: Sí, levántense a las seis.
  Señor Ponce: No, no se levanten a las seis.

1. ¿Nos vestimos?

   Señora Ponce: _____

   Señor Ponce: _____

2. ¿Nos ponemos los zapatos?

   Señora Ponce: _____

   Señor Ponce: _____

3. ¿Nos sentamos a la mesa?

   Señora Ponce: _____

   Señor Ponce: _____

4. ¿Nos preparamos el desayuno?

   Señora Ponce: _____

   Señor Ponce: _____

5. ¿Nos quedamos en la cocina?

   Señora Ponce: _____

   Señor Ponce: _____

6. ¿Nos vamos?

   Señora Ponce: _____

   Señor Ponce: _____

El subjuntivo con deseos y emociones ....

A. Complete each of the sentences below with the appropriate form of the verb, either the indicative or the subjunctive.

1. (es/sea)   Creo que este hotel _____ bueno.

2. (da/dé)   Quiero que Ud. nos _____ una habitación con dos camas.

3. (tiene/tenga)   Es preciso que el cuarto _____ aire acondicionado.

4. (sube/suba)   Deseo que el botones _____ nuestras maletas ahora.

5. (hay/haya)   Veo que _____ dos teléfonos en el cuarto.

6. (hacen/hagan)   Espero que los vecinos no _____ mucho ruido.

7. (traen/traigan)   Prefiero que Uds. nos _____ el desayuno mañana.

8. (firmamos/firmemos) ¿Desea Ud. que _____ el registro?

B. **¡Qué hotel!** Mr. Lara's accomodations are not what he expected. Complete his conversation with the hotel clerk with the correct forms of the verbs in parentheses.

Recepcionista: Buenos días, señor Lara. Espero que Ud. (1. estar) _____ satisfecho con su habitación.

Sr. Lara: ¿¡Satisfecho!? Furioso, mejor dicho. No dormí en toda la noche. Quiero que Uds. me

(2. devolver) _____ mi dinero.

Recepcionista: ¿Cómo? Quiero que Ud. me (3. explicar) _____ lo que pasa. Espero que Ud. no

(4. estar) _____ enojado.

Sr. Lara: Estoy enojadísimo. Este hotel es ruidoso y sus huéspedes son muy desconsiderados.

Recepcionista: Pero señor, recuerde que este (5. ser) _____ un hotel de cuatro estrellas.

Sr. Lara: ¿Qué importancia tienen las estrellas? Uds. no merecen (*deserve*) ni una. Quiero que el

botones (6. bajar) _____ mis maletas ahora.

Recepcionista: ¿No desea Ud. que (nosotros) le (7. dar) _____ otra habitación?

Sr. Lara: No, yo deseo que Uds. (8. llamar) _____ un taxi. También quiero que (Uds.)

me (9. permitir) _____ usar el teléfono para reservar una habitación en otro hotel.

C. **Para hablar en el hotel.** Here are some sentences that you might need to use or might hear when staying at a hotel in Latin America. Select the verb from the list below that best completes each sentence and put it in the correct subjunctive form.

apagar	hacer
despertar	recomendar (ie)
firmar	traer
haber (hay)	venir

1. Es preciso que Uds. _____ el registro.

2. Quiero que la camarera _____ más toallas.

3. Es necesario que los vecinos _____ el televisor.

4. La ducha no funciona. Es urgente que (Uds.) _____ a repararla en seguida.

5. Es importante que (Uds.) me _____ mañana a las siete y media de la mañana.

6. Prefiero que la camarera _____ el cuarto ahora.

7. Deseo que Uds. nos _____ un buen restaurante.

8. Ojalá que _____ cuartos con aire acondicionado.

D. Mr. and Mrs. Benítez are in a hotel room in Acapulco and are telling each other what to do. Using one element from each column, make up at least eight sentences that they might say to each other.

MODELO• • • ➤ **Quiero que repares la maleta.**

Quiero que	reparar	a la recepción
Deseo que	cambiar	más toallas
Prefiero que	marcar	jabón y champú
Espero que	llamar	la maleta
Es preciso que	pedir	la bombilla del baño
	sacar	a la recepción
		el número del restaurante
		la ropa de las maletas
		otro cuarto

1. _____

2. _____

3. _____

4. _____

5. _____

6. _____

7. _____

8. _____

El subjuntivo con expresiones de duda y negación . . . .

A. **¿Cómo es este hotel?** Create questions about an imaginary hotel and then answer each one affirmatively and negatively. Choose between the subjunctive and indicative in each subordinate clause.

MODELO• • • ➤ creer (Ud.)/ser/bueno
¿Cree Ud. que este hotel sea bueno?
Sí, creo que es bueno.
No, no creo que sea bueno.

1. pensar (tú)/ser/caro

_____

_____

_____

2. dudar (Uds.)/tener/piscina

_____

_____

_____

3. creer (Ud.)/estar/cerca del centro

_____

_____

_____

4. es cierto/dar/descuentos

_____

_____

_____

5. es posible/incluir/el desayuno en el precio de la habitación

_____

_____

_____

B. **Primer día en Puerto Vallarta.** Carmen and Sarina are at a luxurious resort in Puerto Vallarta, one of Mexico's Pacific Ocean beach resorts. They are checking out the hotel. Complete their conversation.

MODELO● ● ● ➤ ¿Hay sauna?
   No estoy segura de que <u>haya sauna.</u>

1. —¿Sirven el desayuno en el patio?

   —No creo que _____

2. —¿Todas las habitaciones están alquiladas _(rented)?_

   —Es imposible que _____

3. —Dicen que organizan bailes todas las noches.

   —No es verdad que _____

4. —Creo que el hotel tiene doce restaurantes.

   —Yo no creo que _____

5. —Pasan películas nuevas todos los días.

—Dudo que _____

6. —Podemos llevarnos las toallas.

—No es cierto que _____

Vamos a explorar el ciberespacio . . . .

Hotels. The World Wide Web offers many fascinating sites throughout the Spanish-speaking world dealing with the cultural topics in this lesson. Take a virtual field trip. Go to http://www.harcourtcollege.com/spanish/saludosrecuerdos to discover more.

Lección 10
Las diversiones

Conversación . . . .

A. Vamos a salir. Complete the following conversation between Laura and Felisa by underlining the best completion among the choices given in parentheses.

Laura: ¿Qué quieres hacer esta noche? Pasan una nueva película española en el centro. Podremos ir a verla a las ocho (1. sin que, cuando, a menos que) prefieras hacer otra cosa.

Felisa: Hay un concierto de música clásica en el Teatro Colón. Y, con tal que (2. queden, quedan, quedarán) entradas, podemos invitar a Micaela.

Laura: No creo que Micaela (3. pudo, pueda, podrá) ir. Pasa todo el día pintando. Van a exponer algunos de sus cuadros en una galería de arte del centro.

Felisa: Tienes razón. Mira, aquí en la cartelera *(entertainment listings)* de hoy dice que ponen la obra Don Juan. ¿Por qué no vamos a verla?

Laura: Buena idea. Voy a llamar a la taquilla (4. para que, para, porque) saber cuánto cuestan las entradas.

Felisa: Antes de que (5. llames, llamarás, llamaste) a la taquilla, hablaré con Jaime. A él le encanta (6. el cine, el teatro, la música) y yo estoy segura de que (7. quiera, querrá, quiso) ir con nosotras.

Laura: Muy bien. Llámalo ahora. (8. Tan pronto como, Antes de que, Aunque) sepas cuántos seremos, aparto las entradas.

El futuro . . . .

A. Pensando en el futuro. What will these people do ten years from now? Write a sentence in the future to tell what they will do.

MODELO • • ➤ Lorenzo/escribir obras de teatro ➜
Lorenzo escribirá obras de teatro.

1. Alejandra/pintar una obra maestra

_____

2. yo/actuar en una película

_____

3. Carlos y Francisca/trabajar en el teatro

_____

4. tú/ser un músico famoso

_____

5. tú y yo/vivir de nuestro arte

_____

6. ustedes/componer canciones

_____

B. **¡Salgamos!** Complete the following sentences with the future tense of the verb at the left to find out what these friends will do this Saturday night.

1. (hacer)   Yo sé lo que tú y yo _____ el sábado por la noche.

2. (ir)   (Nosotros) _____ a un concierto.

3. (escoger)   Yo _____ un concierto.

4. (sacar)   Tú _____ las entradas.

5. (salir)   (Nosotros) _____ a comer antes del concierto.

6. (venir)   Mis primos _____ a la sala de conciertos.

7. (escuchar)   Ellos _____ la música con nosotros.

8. (poder)   Todos nosotros _____ tomar un café después.

C. **¿Cómo serán las cosas aquí?** Marisa is spending a week in Buenos Aires and would like to go to the theater. Rewrite her conjectures about going to the theater by changing these sentences to the future of probability.

MODELO•••➤   Probablemente hay muchos teatros en Buenos Aires.
                 Habrá muchos teatros en Buenos Aires.

1. Probablemente va todo el mundo al teatro.

   _____

2. Probablemente ponen obras muy interesantes.

   _____

3. Probablemente son caras las entradas.

   _____

4. El periódico tiene probablemente una buena cartelera.

   _____

5. Probablemente, los teatros están en el centro.

   _____

6. Las taquillas abren probablemente por la tarde.

   _____

El subjuntivo con algunas expresiones adverbiales . . . .

A. **Oraciones.** Form sentences from each string of elements.

MODELO•••➤   Te daré el dinero/para que/(tú)/pagarles la cuenta
                 Te daré el dinero para que les pagues la cuenta.

1. Te daré el dinero/a menos que/(tú)/no necesitarlo

_____

Te daré el dinero/con tal de que/(tú)/devolvérmelo

_____

Te daré el dinero/para que/(tú)/comprarte ropa nueva

_____

Te daré el dinero/sin que/(tú)/pedírmelo

_____

2. Hablaremos con los Martínez/sin que/(nadie)/saberlo

_____

Hablaremos con los Martínez/para que/(ellos)/comprender el asunto

_____

Hablaremos con los Martínez/antes de que/Adela/llamarlos

_____

Hablaremos con los Martínez/a menos que/(ellos)/no querer escucharnos

_____

3. Yo te ayudo con las matemáticas/con tal de que/(tú)/esforzarte *(make an effort)*

_____

Yo te ayudo con las matemáticas/para que/(tú)/sacar una buena nota

_____

Yo te ayudo con las matemáticas/a menos que/(tú)/no querer

_____

Yo te ayudo con las matemáticas/antes de que/el profesor/dar el examen

_____

4. Vamos al museo de arte/a menos que/los chicos/preferir hacer otra cosa

_____

Vamos al museo de arte/sin que/Carolina/saberlo

_____

Vamos al museo de arte/para que/los chicos/ver las obras maestras

_____

Vamos al museo de arte/con tal de que/no ser demasiado tarde

_____

B. Hablando de diversiones. Discuss your plans with a friend by completing these sentences.

1. Iremos al cine a menos que tú _____

_____

2. Saquemos otra entrada para que Juan _____

_____

3. El sábado habrá partido de fútbol con tal de que _____

_____

4. No saldremos sin que los chicos _____

_____

5. Quisiera ver el cuadro que estás pintando antes de que tú _____

_____

El subjuntivo con otras expresiones adverbiales . . . .

A. Siempre así. Complete the following sentences according to the tense of the verb in the main clause.

MODELO● ● ● ➤ Pinto cuando vuelvo del trabajo.
Pintaré cuando vuelva del trabajo.
Pinté cuando volví del trabajo.

1. Lloro cuando veo esa película.

Lloraré cuando _____

Lloré cuando _____

2. Espero hasta que llegan los chicos.

Esperaré hasta que _____

Esperé hasta que _____

3. Salen tan pronto como termina la función.

Saldrán tan pronto como _____

Salieron tan pronto como _____

4. Ayudas a Pablo aunque es difícil.

Ayudarás a Pablo aunque _____

Ayudaste a Pablo aunque _____

B. **¡Teatro!** What would this teacher tell her class about the drama unit they're going to do? Complete her sentences in a logical fashion.

1. Leeremos esta obra aunque _____

_____

2. La representaremos tan pronto como ustedes _____

_____

3. Habrá muchos ensayos *(rehearsals)* hasta que _____

_____

4. Invitaremos a todos los profesores y estudiantes de la facultad cuando _____

_____

Las preposiciones *para* y *por*. . . . .

A. Complete these two accounts of going out to see a play or concert with either **para** or **por.**

A. Salimos (1.) _____ el teatro. Queríamos llegar temprano (2.) _____ comprar las entradas. Yo fui (3.) _____ la tarde a comprar las entradas. Pagué 70 dólares (4.) _____ las dos entradas. Usé mi tarjeta de crédito (5.) _____ pagarlas. Antes de entrar al teatro, dimos un paseo (6.) _____ el barrio.

B. Mi amigo Pedro trabaja (7.) _____ una compañía que presenta conciertos. El sábado viene a cantar un grupo que me gusta mucho. Llamé a Pedro (8.) _____ ver si podía conseguirme dos entradas. Me dijo que me podía conseguir dos, pero que costaban cincuenta dólares (9.) _____ entrada. (10.) _____ lo general no gasto tanto dinero en diversiones, pero este grupo es muy especial. Salí caminando (11.) _____ la casa de Pedro. Cuando saqué el dinero, me dijo Pedro: —Tengo una sorpresa (12.) _____ ti. La compañía me regaló cuatro entradas. (13.) _____ eso no me tienes que pagar. —Gracias (14.) _____ las entradas —le dije. —Eres un gran amigo, Pedro.

Los pronombres con preposiciones . . . .

A. Answer the following questions in the affirmative using the correct form of the pronoun after the preposition.

MODELO•••➤ ¿Este libro es para Gonzalo?
Sí, es para él.

1. ¿Estas entradas son para mí?

_____

2. ¿Hiciste esto por los chicos?

_____

3. ¿Carlos va al cine contigo?

_____

4. ¿Pagaste mucho por aquel cuadro?

_____

5. ¿Su padre influyó mucho en Marcela?

_____

6. ¿Lupe irá sin ustedes?

_____

B. **Éste sí, el otro no.** Clarify things for your friend saying that these things will happen to the first person mentioned, but not to the second. Pay attention to the use of pronouns after prepositions.

MODELO•••➤ ¿Hablarán de Pedro y Clara?
De él, sí. De ella, no.

1. ¿Compraste regalos para mamá y papá?

_____

2. ¿Hablarán conmigo o contigo?

_____

3. ¿Vendrán con Federico y Carla?

_____

4. ¿El profesor se queja de ti o de mí?

_____

5. ¿Tus tíos les dan mucho dinero a sus hijas y a sus nietos?

_____

6. ¿Tus abuelos influyen mucho en ti y en tus hermanos?

_____

Vamos a explorar el ciberespacio . . . .

Entertainment. The World Wide Web offers many fascinating sites throughout the Spanish-speaking world dealing with the cultural topics in this lesson. Take a virtual field trip. Go to http://www.harcourtcollege.com/spanish/saludosrecuerdos to discover more.

Laboratory Manual

Lección preliminar
¡Saludos!

Conversación . . . .

A. Listen to the following conversation between two students, Martín and Teresa, and repeat each sentence in the pauses provided. Then answer the questions below. Based on the dialogue that you have just practiced, tell whether each of the following statements is true or false, or whether you don't have enough information to decide.

1. El chico es Martín.
   a. true   b. false   c. not enough information

2. Teresa está muy bien.
   a. true   b. false   c. not enough information

3. El 5-35-12-23 es el teléfono de Martín.
   a. true   b. false   c. not enough information

4. María Salinas está bastante bien.
   a. true   b. false   c. not enough information

5. Es tarde.
   a. true   b. false   c. not enough information

Cultura . . . .

A. You will hear a description of Mexico read twice. Listen carefully and complete the missing words of the text. Note the words **hay** *(there is, there are)* and **playas** *(beaches)*. Here is a list of the words left out.

capital	Estados	país
ciudad	hay	playas
español	norte	tropicales

México es un país que está al sur de los _____ Unidos. Es un país muy grande con casi cien

millones de habitantes. La _____ de México es la ciudad de México, una _____ muy

grande con veinte millones de personas. En México hablan _____.

México es un _____ muy variado. Tiene costas en el Mar Caribe y en el Océano Pacífico. En

México hay playas famosas, como las _____ de Cancún y Acapulco. En México también

_____ muchas montañas. En el _____ del país hay desiertos como en el suroeste de

los Estados Unidos. En el sur de México, hay selvas *(jungles)* _____.

Alfabeto . . . .

A. **Las vocales.** Listen to the following words, paying special attention to the pronunciation of the vowels. Repeat each one after the speaker.

¡Saludos! Laboratory Manual—Lección preliminar

1. **La letra** *a* as in *father:* Ana, la casa, la sala, la banana

2. **La letra** *e* as in *bet:* me, te, le, ese, Elena, está

3. **La letra** *i* as in *machine:* sí, Misisipí, mío, chico

4. **La letra** *o* as in *note:* ¿cómo?, foto, loco, solo, dos

5. **La letra** *u* as in *rule:* tú, uno, mucho, Cuba, gusta

B. **Diphthongs.** A diphthong is a combination of any two vowels that includes i (y) or u, or a combination of i/u/y, and is pronounced as a single syllable. Repeat the following words after the speaker.

1. seis		**6.** gracias	
2. bueno		**7.** cuidar	
3. siete		**8.** ciudad	
4. hay		**9.** ley	
5. luego		**10.** agua	

C. **More Diphthongs.** Each of the following words contains a diphthong. Repeat each after the speaker and underline the diphthong.

MODELO• • • ➤ You hear: bueno
You write: b<u>ue</u>no

1. cuatro

2. muy

3. diez

4. adiós

5. treinta

6. nueve

D. **El alfabeto.** Repeat the names of the letters of the Spanish alphabet after the speaker.

a	a	j	jota	r	ere
b	be	k	ka	rr**	erre
c	ce	l	ele	s	ese
ch*	che	ll*	elle	t	te
d	de	m	eme	u	u
e	e	n	ene	v	ve (uve)
f	efe	ñ	eñe	w	doble v
g	ge	o	o	x	equis
h	hache	p	pe	y	i griega
i	i	q	cu	z	zeta

* Was eliminated as an official letter of the Spanish alphabet in 1994.
** Not an official letter of the Spanish alphabet.

E. Listen to each word and spell it out letter by letter. The speaker will give the correct spelling afterwards.

1. casa

2. luz

3. soy

4. tenis

5. reloj

6. bien

7. señor

Números 0–99...

A. The speaker will read each of these people's phone number. Write the phone number out in figures.

1. Evita González _____

2. Fernán Molina _____

3. Samuel Ordóñez _____

4. Jacinto Tello _____

5. Luisa Osorio _____

Lección 1
La clase y las presentaciones

Conversación . . . .

A. You're working in an office in Mexico City. Two colleagues are introducing themselves to each other. Listen to their conversation and read along.

Sr. Ortega: Buenos días. Me llamo Carlos Ortega. ¿Cómo se llama usted?

Srta. Peña: Me llamo Isabel Peña.

Sr. Ortega: Mucho gusto, señorita.

Srta. Peña: El gusto es mío, señor Ortega.

B. Following the pattern you have just heard, introduce yourself to Isabel Peña. The speaker will take the role of Isabel Peña. Say the missing lines and write them in the spaces provided.

Usted: _____

Srta. Peña: Me llamo Isabel Peña.

Usted: _____

Srta. Peña: El gusto es mío.

Pronunciación. . . . .

A. Repeat each word after the speaker. Note that the letters **b** and **v** both represent the sound /b/ at the beginning of a word (after a pause).

bueno/ventana   Bolivia/Venezuela
bien/veinte   Bárbara/Víctor
bastante/videocasetera   bolígrafo/vosotros
baloncesto/vóleibol

Pronouns. . . . .

A. Repeat each of these sentences after the speaker. Then, when you hear the cue **Cambie** (*Change*), say the sentence again, replacing the noun subject with the appropriate pronoun: **él, ella, nosotros, ellos, ellas, ustedes.** You will hear a confirmation of the correct response.

MODELO• • • ➤   Juan es abogado.
                ➔ Él es abogado.

1. María es de España.

2. Teresa y Rosa son cantantes.

3. Vicente y tú son de Puerto Rico.

4. Ramón y yo somos estudiantes.

5. Víctor es cubano.

6. Julio y Elena son de México.

Ser ·

A. **¿Quiénes son estas personas?** Use the cues you will hear (they are written below) to describe each person. Use the verb **ser.** Each description will consist of two sentences, the first telling what the people do and the second where they are from. You will hear a confirmation of the correct response.

> **MODELO**• • • ➤ Julia/cantante/Puerto Rico.
> Julia es cantante. Es de Puerto Rico.

1. tú/turista/España

2. Julio y Marcos/actores/Colombia

3. yo/estudiante/Estados Unidos

4. María y Luisa/doctoras/Cuba

5. tú y yo/compañeros/México

6. Vicente/programador/Nicaragua

El salón de clase ·

A. The speaker will say a number that refers to an object in the drawing. The speaker will then ask you a question about that object. In each case you will answer with two sentences, one saying that the object is NOT what the speaker asked, the second sentence telling what the object is. Follow the models and note that **es** is used with singular nouns and **son** with plural nouns.

Número 1. ¿Es el escritorio?
No, no es el escritorio. Es la pizarra.

Número 2. ¿Son los papeles?
No, no son los papeles. Son los mapas.

_____

_____

_____

_____

_____

_____

_____

Dictado. . . . .

A. Listen carefully as Víctor Romero introduces himself. Write down what you hear during each pause. Each word group will be read twice. The entire passage will then be repeated without pauses for you to check your work. Use question and exclamation marks where appropriate.

_____

_____

_____

_____

_____

_____

_____

_____

Lección 2
La familia y las descripciones

Descripciones ....

A. Listen as you read along to Isabel, Santiago, and Federico's descriptions of themselves.

Me llamo Isabel Ruiz de Torres. Soy de San Antonio, Texas. Soy casada. Mi esposo se llama Alfredo Torres. Alfredo y yo somos estudiantes aquí en San Antonio. Yo estudio lenguas y literatura, y Alfredo estudia química. Me gusta mucho la ciudad de San Antonio por sus tradiciones hispanas y norteamericanas. Alfredo y yo deseamos comprar una casa en San Antonio.

Soy venezolano. Me llamo Santiago Delgado y Oliva. Soy ingeniero. Trabajo en la compañía Petróleos Nacionales de Venezuela. Hablo inglés y español. Me gustan mucho los deportes y participo en un equipo de fútbol. Soy socio del Club Cívico de mi ciudad. Mi novia[1] se llama Alicia Cárdenas. Ella estudia informática en la universidad.

Soy el doctor Federico Fajardo-Silva. Enseño medicina en la Universidad Nacional de México. También trabajo en un hospital muy grande. Estoy siempre muy ocupado. Me gusta mucho mi profesión. Soy casado con dos hijos. Mi hijo mayor desea estudiar medicina. El otro desea estudiar economía y trabajar en un banco.

[1] **la novia** *girl friend*

B. Now listen again and repeat during each pause.

C. Now answer the true/false questions. Circle **C** for **cierto** *(true)* and **F** for **falso** *(false).*

1. Isabel estudia lenguas y literatura.	C	F
2. Isabel es soltera.	C	F
3. Isabel y su esposo estudian en México.	C	F
4. Santiago trabaja para una compañía venezolana.	C	F
5. Santiago habla italiano y francés.	C	F
6. Isabel Ruiz es la novia de Santiago.	C	F
7. El doctor Fajardo-Silva enseña y trabaja en un hospital también.	C	F
8. Uno de los hijos del doctor Fajardo-Silva es abogado y el otro es profesor.	C	F

D. Ud. busca trabajo. You are at an employment agency. The interviewer asks you the following questions. Repeat each question after the speaker and then answer it in a complete sentence in the pause provided. Possible answers will be given by the speaker.

1. ¿Cómo se llama Ud.?

2. ¿Habla Ud. español?

3. ¿Es Ud. de Venezuela?

4. ¿Estudia Ud. en la universidad?

5. ¿Trabaja Ud. ahora?

6. ¿Es Ud. soltero? ¿Es Ud. soltera?

Pronunciación. . . . .

A. Practice pronouncing the Spanish **r**'s. First repeat these words with single **r** after the speaker. The speaker will model each word twice and you will repeat the word each time you hear it :

espero	turista
miro	hermano
soltero	compra
derecha	madre
para	padre
primo	preocupado

B. Now repeat these words with double **r** or trilled **r** after the speaker.

correr	Rosa
corro	recto
aburrido	Roberto
cerrado	rico
correo	Rafael
pizarra	reloj

La familia . . . .

A. Listen to the description of Pablito Ortega's family. The speaker will read it twice. Look at the family tree as you listen. Then the speaker will ask you questions about Pablito's family. Answer each question **sí** or **no** in a complete sentence. Then repeat the correct response after the speaker. Refer, when necessary, to the family tree.

Listen to the description.

La familia de Pablito Ortega es bastante grande. Hay abuelos, tíos y primas. La familia de Pablito es de México, pero los abuelos Linares, los padres de la madre de Pablito, son de España. Los padres de Pablito son profesores. Enseñan en la universidad. El tío Antonio estudia medicina y el tío Marcos trabaja en una oficina. Los dos tíos son muy inteligentes y muy trabajadores. La tía Ana María es artista. Trabaja en casa. Las primas de Pablito son muy simpáticas.

Now, answer the questions. You will hear each question once:

MODELO• • • ➤   You hear: ¿La tía Ana María es profesora?
                          You see: tía Ana María/artista
                          You say: No, la tía Ana María es artista.

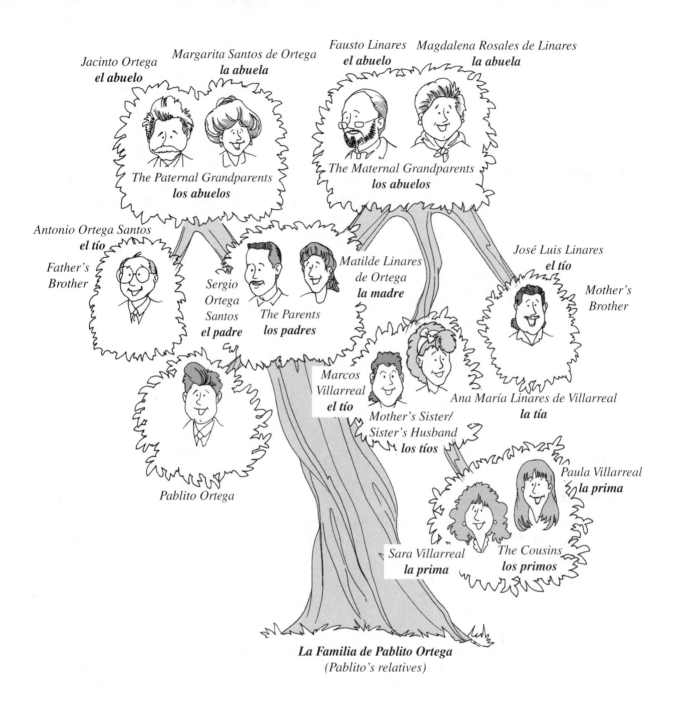

Jacinto Ortega
el abuelo

Margarita Santos de Ortega
la abuela

Fausto Linares
el abuelo

Magdalena Rosales de Linares
la abuela

The Paternal Grandparents
los abuelos

The Maternal Grandparents
los abuelos

Antonio Ortega Santos
el tío

Father's Brother

Sergio Ortega Santos
el padre

The Parents
los padres

Matilde Linares de Ortega
la madre

José Luis Linares
el tío

Mother's Brother

Marcos Villarreal
el tío

Mother's Sister/ Sister's Husband
los tíos

Ana María Linares de Villarreal
la tía

Pablito Ortega

Paula Villarreal
la prima

Sara Villarreal
la prima

The Cousins
los primos

La Familia de Pablito Ortega
(Pablito's relatives)

1. familia de Pablito Ortega/bastante grande

2. abuelos Linares/de España

3. madre de Pablito/profesora

4. tíos/inteligentes

5. primas/muy simpáticas

Dictado . . . .

A. Listen carefully to the passage about Pablito's family and write down what you hear during each pause. Each word group will be read twice. The entire passage will then be repeated without pauses for you to check your work. Now let's begin.

_____

_____

_____

_____

_____

_____

_____

_____

_____

B. Now translate the description you have just written into English.

_____

_____

_____

_____

_____

_____

_____

_____

_____

_____

Descripciones . . . .

A. Have a conversation with the speaker about what certain people are like. The speaker will describe one person and ask you about the other. You describe the second person as being the opposite of the first. Listen to the model.

MODELO • • • ➤ You hear: Marta es trabajadora. ¿Y Pedro?
        You say: Pedro es perezoso.

B. Say whether or not these are typical activities in the Spanish class. Answer the speaker's questions in the pauses provided. The speaker will confirm the correct response. Listen to the model.

MODELO• • • ➤   You hear: ¿Hablas español?
You reply: Sí, hablo español.

You hear: ¿Cocina la profesora espaguetis?
You reply: No, la profesora no cocina espaguetis.

Ser y estar . . . .

A. **Mi familia.** Sonia is talking about her family. Use the cues you hear to create full sentences to find out what she says. You will have to choose between **ser** and **estar** in each case. The speaker will confirm the correct response. Listen to the model.

MODELO• • • ➤   You hear: mi familia/muy grande
You say: Mi familia es muy grande.

B. **Lógico o ilógico.** The speaker will read some statements to you. In each case, mark whether the statement is logical (**lógico**) or illogical (**ilógico**). You will hear each statement twice. Follow the model.

MODELO• • • ➤   You hear: María está enferma. Está en el hospital.
You mark: *lógico.*

1.   _____ lógico   _____ ilógico

2.   _____ lógico   _____ ilógico

3.   _____ lógico   _____ ilógico

4.   _____ lógico   _____ ilógico

5.   _____ lógico   _____ ilógico

6.   _____ lógico   _____ ilógico

Lección 3
Las comidas

Conversación ....

A. Lucía has gone out to eat. Listen to her conversation with the waiter as you read along. Then answer the questions that follow. You will hear the conversation again after doing the questions so that you can check your work.

Mesero:	Buenas tardes. ¿Qué desea Ud., señorita?
Lucía:	¡Hay tantos platos deliciosos en el menú! Me gustan tantas cosas que veo en la lista. Bueno, primero, la sopa de cebolla.
Mesero:	Bien. ¿Y después?
Lucía:	Creo que el pollo, con papas y verduras.
Mesero:	¿Desea una ensalada también?
Lucía:	Buena idea. Una ensalada de lechuga y tomates.
Mesero:	Perfecto. ¿Y para tomar?
Lucía:	Agua mineral con la comida. Después, café.
Mesero:	Tenemos muchas tortas deliciosas. Preparamos las tortas aquí en la cocina del restaurante.
Lucía:	Ay, no sé si debo comer postres. Bueno, voy a ver después de la comida. Ah, y veo que no hay cuchillo aquí.
Mesero:	Muy bien, señorita. Regreso con su cuchillo y su sopa.

The following statements are false. Correct them according to the conversation between Lucía and the waiter.

1. Lucía cree que hay pocas cosas buenas en el menú.

_____

2. Lucía va a comer una sopa de frijoles.

_____

3. Después va a comer carne y arroz.

_____

4. No desea ensalada.

_____

5. Va a tomar vino con la comida.

_____

6. No hay torta en el restaurante.

_____

7. No hay tenedor en la mesa de Lucía.

_____

8. Después de la comida, Lucía toma té.

Pronunciación. . . . .

A. *s, z, ce, ci*. Practice pronouncing the Spanish **s.** In Latin American Spanish, this sound is represented by the letters **s, z,** and **c** before **e** and **i.** Repeat these words after the speaker. The speaker will model each word twice and you will repeat the word each time you hear it.

s	z	ce, ci
sal	taza	cebolla
saber	manzana	conoce
queso	marzo	hace
vaso	arroz	recibir
mesas	maíz	diciembre
papas	feliz	cocina

El verbo *ir*. . . . .

A. Ask if these people are going to the places indicated. The speaker will confirm the correct response.

> **MODELO• • • ➤** You see: el restaurante
> You hear: Teresa
> You say: **¿Va al restaurante?**

1. la biblioteca

2. la cafetería

3. el gimnasio

4. la oficina

5. la universidad

B. **El fin de semana.** Tell what people are going to do this weekend using **ir a** + infinitive. The speaker will confirm the correct response.

> **MODELO• • • ➤** You see and hear: comer en un restaurante/ustedes
> You say: **Ustedes van a comer en un restaurante.**

1. estudiar/yo

2. cocinar/mi mamá

3. jugar al fútbol/mis amigos

4. comprar una computadora/Carmen

5. escuchar música/tú

El presente de los verbos *-er/-ir*. . . . .

A. Answer the following questions affirmatively or negatively, as indicated. You will hear each question twice. The speaker will confirm the correct response.

MODELO• • •➤ You hear: ¿Qué lees? ¿El libro de español? ¿Qué lees? ¿El libro de español?
　　　　　　　You see: Sí,...
　　　　　　　You say: **Sí, leo el libro de español.**

　　　　　　　You hear: ¿Dónde vives? ¿En la ciudad? ¿Dónde vives? ¿En la ciudad?
　　　　　　　You see: No,...
　　　　　　　You say: **No, no vivo en la ciudad.**

Begin.

1. Sí,...

2. No,...

3. Sí,...

4. No,...

5. Sí,...

6. No,...

La *a* personal . . . .

A. Whom and what are these people seeing? Construct sentences with the verb **ver** and the elements you see and hear, using the personal **a** where necessary. The speaker will confirm the correct response.

MODELO• • •➤ You see and hear: Tomás/María
　　　　　　　You say: **Tomás ve a María.**

1. mis amigos/un programa de televisión

2. María/sus tíos

3. Rosario y Sara/el mesero

4. Eduardo/la nueva película (*film*)

5. nosotros/Daniela

6. tú/tus compañeros

Las días . . . .

A. Say the day that follows the one you hear. The speaker will confirm the correct response. Follow the model.

MODELO• • •➤ You hear: Hoy es lunes.
　　　　　　　You say: **Mañana es martes.**

1. ...

2. ...

3. ...

4. ...

5. ...

Los meses..

A. Each of these people's birthdays is one month earlier than the speaker thinks. Tell the speaker in which month their birthday falls. The speaker will confirm the correct response. Follow the model.

MODELO • • • ➤ You hear: El cumpleaños de tu papá es en febrero, ¿verdad?
    You say: **No, es en enero.**

1. ...

2. ...

3. ...

4. ...

5. ...

Dictado..

A. Alicia Delgado tells about a potluck supper she and her friends are organizing for Saturday night. Write down what she says during each pause. Alicia will say each phrase twice and then will repeat the entire passage without pauses for you to check your work.

_____

_____

_____

_____

_____

_____

_____

_____

_____

_____

B. Now translate into English the passage you have just heard.

_____

_____

Lección 4
Las actividades diarias

Conversación . . . .

A. **El horario de clases.** Felipe and Sara are talking about Felipe's class schedule. Listen to their conversation as you read along.

Sara: ¿A qué hora te levantas los lunes?
Felipe: A las seis y media.
Sara: ¡Tan temprano! ¿Por qué?
Felipe: Porque a las ocho tengo la clase de historia con el profesor Dávila. Es un profesor fantástico y me gusta mucho su clase.
Sara: El profesor Dávila da mucho trabajo, ¿no?
Felipe: Sí, hay que leer mucho. Pero los libros son muy interesantes.
Sara: ¿Y a qué hora almuerzas?
Felipe: A la una, en la cafetería. ¿Quieres venir?
Sara: Con mucho gusto. Yo también almuerzo a la una.

B. Now listen again and repeat after the speakers.

C. The speaker will read some false statements about the conversation between Felipe and Sara. Correct each one orally. You will hear each statement twice. The speaker will confirm the correct answer.

1. …

2. …

3. …

4. …

5. …

Pronunciación. . . . .

A. ***j, ge, gi, qu.*** Practice pronouncing these Spanish consonants. Repeat these words containing Spanish **j** or **g** before **e** and **i** after the speaker. The speaker will model each word twice and you will repeat the word each time you hear it.

joven	biología
juntos	gimnasio
trabajo	generalmente
ejercicio	gente
jugar	región
jueves	página

Now practice these words containing the combination of letters **qu.** The speaker will model each word twice and you will repeat the word each time you hear it.

queso	quito	quince	quien	que

Los adjetivos posesivos. . . . .

A. **¡Listos para la clase!** All the students have what they need on the first day of school. Say so by using the cues that you hear to form sentences with the verb **tener** and the appropriate possessive adjective. Follow the model. The speaker will confirm the correct response.

> **MODELO** • • • ➤   You hear: Luisa/lápiz
> You say: Luisa tiene su lápiz.

1. Martín/bolígrafo

2. todos los estudiantes/cuadernos

3. nosotros/libros

4. tú/calculadora

5. yo/horario

6. tú y yo/computadoras

B. **Para ser preciso.** Use a phrase beginning with **de** + the definite article to specify exactly which thing you mean. Follow the model. The speaker will confirm the correct response.

> **MODELO** • • • ➤   You hear: ¿Qué libro lees?
> la estudiante
> You say: El libro de la estudiante.

1. ¿Qué foto quieres ver? / el niño

2. ¿Qué restaurante es bueno? / el señor Morales

3. ¿Qué carro manejas? / la hermana de Carlos

4. ¿Qué examen tienes hoy? / el profesor Sánchez

5. ¿Qué casa te gusta? / los vecinos

6. ¿Qué verduras son buenas? / el mercado

Verbos con cambios radicales e → ie, o → ue. . . . .

A. **¿Qué hacen hoy?** Use the cues to tell what these students are doing today. Create a complete sentence in each case. Follow the model. The speaker will confirm the correct response.

> **MODELO** • • • ➤   You hear: Vicente/jugar al tenis
> You say: Vicente juega al tenis.

1. tú y yo/almorzar en un restaurante

2. Margarita/almorzar en casa

3. yo/volver a la universidad

4. papá y mamá/querer salir

5. tú/empezar a estudiar

6. mi perro/dormir

B. Yo también. Say that you are doing everything the speaker says. Follow the model. The speaker will confirm the correct response.

MODELO• • • ➤   You hear: Mis amigos y yo estudiamos español.
You say: Yo estudio español también.

1. ...   **2.** ...   **3.** ...   **4.** ...   **5.** ...   **6.** ...

Los verbos reflexivos ....

A. La familia Durán. It's a busy morning at the Durán family's house. Help Mariana Durán tell what each member of the family is doing by forming sentences from the cues you hear. Follow the model. The speaker will confirm the correct response.

MODELO• • • ➤   You hear: mi hermano Carlos/levantarse
You say: Mi hermano Carlos se levanta.

1. ...   **3.** ...   **5.** ...   **7.** ...

2. ...   **4.** ...   **6.** ...   **8.** ...

La hora ....

A. ¿A qué hora es? The speaker will make a series of statements based on Diana's schedule. If the statement is correct, circle **sí**; if it is wrong, circle **no**.

1. sí   no

2. sí   no

3. sí   no

4. sí   no

5. sí   no

6. sí   no

7. sí   no

8. sí   no

	Guadalajara, México **VIERNES 30 DE ABRIL**
8:10	*tomar el autobús*
9:00	*clase de comunicaciones*
10:00	*ver a Teresa en la biblioteca*
12:30	*almuerzo con Guillermo*
2:00	*clase de gimnasio*
4:00	*volver a casa y hacer la tarea*
7:00	*cena con la familia*
9:00	*concierto con Laura y Bárbara*

B. ¡Escuche, por favor! The speaker will ask questions or make a statement. Read the responses suggested and underline the correct answer in each case. First listen to the model.

MODELO• • • ➤   You hear: Necesitamos comprar comida para la cena.
You read: a. Vamos a la iglesia, entonces.
b. Vamos al mercado, entonces.
c. Vamos a la farmacia, entonces.
d. Vamos a la biblioteca, entonces.
You underline response *b* .

1. a. Te levantas a las doce.
   b. Me levanto en cinco minutos.
   c. Me levanto a las diez y media.
   d. Nos levantamos a las nueve.

2. a. Me despierto temprano.
   b. Me preparo un sándwich.
   c. Me pongo la ropa.
   d. Me afeito.

3. a. Y yo no tengo tiempo.
   b. Voy en cinco minutos.
   c. Creo que es a las dos.
   d. Son las doce.

4. a. Me llamo Joaquín Aranda.
   b. Sánchez. Se llama Rodolfo Sánchez.
   c. Podemos llamar al profesor.
   d. Te llamas Alfredo, ¿verdad?

5. a. Porque sus amigos están allí y van a divertirse mucho.
   b. Porque mis amigos están allí y voy a divertirme mucho.
   c. Porque tus amigos están allí y vas a divertirte mucho.
   d. Porque ya están en el café.

6. a. ¿Qué dices? José no se enoja con el profesor.
   b. El profesor Delgado no se enoja.
   c. Yo también estoy muy enojado contigo.
   d. José siempre se duerme en la clase.

7. a. Debes jugar al fútbol.
   b. Debes trabajar más.
   c. Debes acostarte.
   d. Debes ir al gimnasio.

8. a. Me baño, me pongo la ropa y voy.
   b. ¿Por qué no se maquilla?
   c. Oh, sí. Mañana salimos.
   d. No sé si están listos o no.

Lección 5
La salud y el cuerpo

Conversación . . . .

A. Listen to the dialogue as you read along.

La señora Matilde Acevedo de Galíndez lleva a sus dos hijos Carlos y Paula a ver a la doctora Ermelinda Salinas. Carlos tiene cinco años y Paula tiene nueve.

Dra. Salinas:	Buenos días. ¿Qué tienen sus hijos, señora?
Carlos:	Yo tengo tos *ahemm ahemm* y estornudo mucho. Pero no necesito una inyección.
Sra. Acevedo:	Carlitos, por favor. Doctora, los dos están tosiendo y se quejan de dolores de cabeza.
Paula:	Yo tengo dolor de oídos también. Y no puedo respirar bien. Tengo miedo. Tengo mucho miedo.
Sra. Acevedo:	Paula, ¿por qué tan dramática? Estamos en una clínica, y no en un teatro.
Dra. Salinas:	¿Tienen fiebre?
Sra. Acevedo:	Muy poca.
Dra. Salinas:	Chicos, necesito examinarles la garganta y los oídos.
Sra. Acevedo:	¿Qué cree Ud. que tienen, doctora?
Dra. Salinas:	Creo que los dos tienen gripe. Hay muchos chicos enfermos de la gripe ahora.
Sra. Acevedo:	¿Necesitan antibióticos?
Dra. Salinas:	Por ahora, no. Necesitan descansar y tomar mucho jugo para el dolor. Si no mejoran, les voy a recetar un antibiótico.
Carlos y Paula:	Entonces, ¡no podemos ir a la escuela! ¡Vamos a quedarnos en casa viendo televisión!
Sra. Acevedo:	Chicos, yo voy a llamar a sus profesores y preguntar qué tarea tienen. Mientras están descansando, pueden hacerla.
Carlos y Paula:	¡Ay, mamá!

B. The speaker will make a statement about the dialogue. If the statement is true, put an *X* next to **C, cierto;** if it is false, put an *X* next to **F, falso.** If no information has been provided, put an *X* next to the question marks. First listen to the model.

MODELO• • • ➤ You hear: Ermelinda Salinas es la doctora.
You see and mark: C _X_ F ____ ¿? ____

1. C _____   F _____   ¿? _____

2. C _____   F _____   ¿? _____

3. C _____   F _____   ¿? _____

4. C _____   F _____   ¿? _____

5. C _____   F _____   ¿? _____

6. C _____   F _____   ¿? _____

7. C _____   F _____   ¿? _____

8. C _____   F _____   ¿? _____

C. **¡Un accidente!** A bus has skidded off the road. No one is seriously hurt, but people have a lot of aches and pains. To find out where the passengers were injured, listen to the following sentences and complete them according to what you hear. Make sure to include the definite article when you hear it. You will hear each sentence twice.

1. Martín tiene dolor de _____.

2. A mí me duelen _____.

3. Susana no puede mover _____.

4. Jorge tiene sangre en _____.

5. Ana y Rosa tienen problemas con _____.

6. Luis tiene dolor de _____.

7. A ti te duelen _____.

Verbos con cambios radicales e → i ....

A. **¡Ay, qué catarro!** Everyone is asking for medicine for their colds. Tell about this by restating the lead sentence with each new subject. First listen to the model.

MODELO • • ➤   You hear: Bárbara pide medicina.
           You repeat: Bárbara pide medicina.
           You hear: los estudiantes
           You say: Los estudiantes piden medicina.

1. ....   **2.** ....   **3.** ....   **4.** ....   **5.** ....   **6.** ....

Expresiones con *tener* ....

A. Say aloud which of the two sentences given matches the statements you hear. First listen to the model. The speaker will confirm the correct response.

MODELO • • ➤   You hear: Tengo muchas ganas de dormir.
           You see: Tienes sed./Tienes sueño.
           You say: Tienes sueño.

1. Tiene prisa./Tiene cuidado.

2. Tienes frío./Tienes dolor de cabeza.

3. Tengo ganas de verlo./Tengo miedo de verlo.

4. Sí, tenemos hambre./Sí, tenemos calor.

5. Sí, ya tiene seis años./Sí, tiene mucha prisa.

6. No, todos tienen sed./No, todos tienen frío.

El presente progresivo ....

A. **¡Esta gripe no termina!** Raquel is asking Sarita questions about her flu. Sarita answers each of the questions in the present progressive to emphasize that the actions asked about are going on right now. Play the role of Sarita and answer Raquel's questions. The speaker will confirm the correct response.

MODELO• • • ➤   You hear: ¿Descansas?
                        You answer: Sí, estoy descansando.

1. ....   **2.** ....   **3.** ....   **4.** ....   **5.** ....   **6.** ....

Los pronombres de complemento directo . . . .

G. Use **me** or **te** to answer these questions. Follow the models. The speaker will confirm the correct response.

MODELO• • • ➤   You hear: ¿Me entiendes?
                        You see: sí
                        You answer: Sí, te entiendo.
                        You hear: ¿Te entiendo bien?
                        You see: no
                        You answer: No, no me entiendes bien.

1. (sí)...   **2.** (sí)...   **3.** (no)...   **4.** (no)...   **5.** (sí)...   **6.** (no)...

B. Now redo exercise A. in the plural. Use **nos** or **los** or **las** to answer these questions. Follow the models. The speaker will confirm the correct response.

MODELO• • • ➤   You hear: ¿Nos entienden Uds.?
                        You see: sí
                        You answer: Sí, las entendemos.
                        You hear: ¿Los entendemos bien?
                        You see: no
                        You answer: No, no nos entienden bien.

1. (sí)...   **2.** (sí)...   **3.** (no)...   **4.** (no)...   **5.** (sí)...   **6.** (no)...

C. **¿Por qué no?** Your friend is telling you several things he is NOT doing. Ask him why not using direct object pronouns in your answers. Follow the model. The speaker will confirm the correct response.

MODELO• • • ➤   You hear: No llamo a Margarita.
                        You answer: ¿Por qué no la llamas?

1. .....   **2.** .....   **3.** .....   **4.** .....   **5.** .....   **6.** .....

Dictado. . . . .

A. Carlota is a college student who lives in a dorm with two roommates. She's having an especially difficult time now. To find out what the problem is, write down what Carlota says during each pause. Each sentence or phrase will be read twice. Carlota's lines will then be repeated without pauses for you to check your work.

_____

_____

_____

_____

_____

_____

_____

_____

_____

_____

_____

_____

_____

_____

_____

_____

Lección 6

En la tienda de ropa

Conversación . . . .

A. Listen and read along as two women compare stores in Venezuela and the United States.

Graciela:	En Nueva York yo iba a muchas tiendas de ropa.
Consuelo:	¿Cómo eran?
Graciela:	Eran muy bonitas y había mucha variedad. Y los almacenes tenían mucha ropa para damas y caballeros.
Consuelo:	¿Y los precios? Me imagino que todo costaba mucho.
Graciela:	No creas. Los precios eran más bajos que aquí en Venezuela. Y siempre había rebajas *(sale, reduction)* donde casi regalaban las cosas.
Consuelo:	No me digas. Seguro que tenías ganas de comprar muchas cosas.
Graciela:	Ah, sí. Quería comprar cientos de cosas: vestidos, faldas, blusas, zapatos, bolsas de cuero.... Pero no tenía suficiente dinero.
Consuelo:	La próxima vez, vamos juntas. Con nuestras tarjetas de crédito, podemos comprar toda la ropa que necesitamos.
Graciela:	¡Y también unas maletas para llevar las cosas a casa!

B. Now repeat the sentences of the dialogue after the speakers.

C. The speaker will make a statement about the dialogue. If the statement is true, put an *X* next to **C, cierto**; if it is false, put an *X* next to **F, falso**. First listen to the model.

MODELO• • • ➤ You hear: Graciela y Consuelo son venezolanas.
You see and mark: C _____X_____ F _____

1. C _____   F _____

2. C _____   F _____

3. C _____   F _____

4. C _____   F _____

5. C _____   F _____

6. C _____   F _____

Adjectivos y pronombres demostrativos . . . .

A. You are at the Corte Inglés department store in Madrid and the clerk is asking you, the customer, if you like certain items. In each case you say that you don't like the ones he's showing you, but the other ones. Use the appropriate demonstrative adjectives and pronouns, as in the model. The speaker will confirm the correct response.

MODELO• • • ➤ You hear: ¿Le gustan estos calcetines?
You say: **¿Ésos? No tanto. Me gustan más los otros.**

1. .....   **2.** .....   **3.** .....   **4.** .....   **5.** .....

Imperfecto...

A. Antes las vacaciones eran diferentes. Answer the speaker's questions by saying that you and your family used to do these things. Use the word **antes** and the imperfect in your answer. The speaker will ask each question twice and will confirm the correct response. First listen to the model.

MODELO• • • ➤ You hear: ¿Pasan Uds. las vacaciones en el campo?
You say: **Ahora no. Antes pasábamos las vacaciones en el campo.**

1. .....   **3.** .....   **5.** .....   **7.** .....

2. .....   **4.** .....   **6.** .....   **8.** .....

Los pronombres de complemento indirecto ....

A. Isabel knows her roommate Margarita is forgetful, so she is checking to see if Margarita is sending out everything she is supposed to. Play the role of Isabel using the verb **enviar** and the necessary indirect object pronouns. The speaker will confirm the correct response. First listen to the model.

MODELO• • • ➤ You hear and see: la tarjeta/tus primos
You say: **¿Les mandas la tarjeta a tus primos?**

1. una carta/Roberto

2. un regalo/tus abuelos

3. los cincuenta dólares/Carlota

4. las fotos/tus padres

5. una sudadera/tu hermano menor

B. Preguntas y respuestas. Listen to each question, then choose the best answer, underline it, and read it aloud. The speaker will confirm the correct response. You will hear each question twice. First listen to the model.

MODELO• • • ➤ You hear: ¿Quién te regala ropa?
You see and say: a. Le regala ropa a mi mamá.
b. <u>Me regala ropa mi mamá.</u>
c. Te regala ropa mi mamá.

1. a. Ud. me prestaba el libro.
   b. Nora me prestaba el libro.
   c. Le prestaba el libro a Nora.

2. a. Mis amigos me escriben a mí.
   b. Te escriben mis amigos.
   c. Les escribe Alicia del Castillo.

3. a. Me pide cien dólares.
   b. No le pido dinero a Carlos.
   c. Le pido cien dólares a Carlos.

4. a. Amalia me va a dar el perfume.
   b. Le voy a dar el perfume a Amalia.
   c. Te va a dar el perfume Amalia.

5. a. Nos compraban ropa nuestros padres.
   b. Les comprábamos ropa a nuestros padres.
   c. Les comprábamos ropa a Uds.

C. A nadie le gusta esta ropa. Say that the reason people are not buying the items of clothing asked about is that they don't like them. The speaker will confirm the correct response. First listen to the model.

MODELO•••➤ You hear: ¿Luisa no va a comprar esa blusa?
    You say: No, no le gusta.

1. ..... **2.** ..... **3.** ..... **4.** ..... **5.** .....

D. Hablando de ropa. Use the cues given and the verb **parecer** with an indirect object pronoun to tell why people like or don't like the items of clothing. The speaker will confirm the correct response. First listen to the model.

MODELO•••➤ You hear: ¿A Marta le gustan estos zapatos?
    You see: sí/bonitos
    You say: Sí, le parecen bonitos.

1. no/fea

2. no/pequeño

3. sí/elegantes

4. no/caras

5. sí/fantástico

¡Escuche, por favor!...............................

A. Buscándose un vestido. Mrs. Lares needs a dress for an elegant party she is invited to. She goes to an exclusive boutique. Preview the statements that follow, and then listen to the conversation between Mrs. Lares and the salesclerk. Mark the statements true or false according to what Mrs. Lares and the salesclerk say. You will hear the conversation twice.

Dependienta:	Mire este vestido negro, señora. Es sencillo, pero elegante. Y me parece que el negro le va a quedar muy bien.
Señora Lares:	Me gusta el color negro. ¿Puedo probarme el vestido?
Dependienta:	Cómo no. Los probadores están a la derecha.
	(Unos minutos después)
Señora Lares:	¿Qué le parece?
Dependienta:	Sabía que le iba a quedar muy bien. Es el vestido ideal para Ud.
Señora Lares:	Me encanta el vestido. Es exactamente lo que yo quería. ¿Cuánto cuesta, señorita?
Dependienta:	Mil doscientos dólares.
Señora Lares:	¡Mil doscientos dólares! Pensaba que era un vestido caro, pero, ¡mil doscientos dólares!
Dependienta:	Es de seda, señora.
Señora Lares:	De seda, pero no de oro.
Dependienta:	Nosotros aceptamos tarjetas de crédito, señora.
Señora Lares:	No sé, no sé, señorita. Tengo que pensarlo un poco.

1. La dependienta le enseña a la señora Lares una falda negra. C   F

2. La señora Lares se prueba el vestido. C   F

3. Los probadores están a la izquierda. C   F

4. El vestido le queda apretado.   C   F

5. El vestido le parece muy caro a la señora Lares.   C   F

6. El vestido cuesta tanto porque es de oro.   C   F

7. La señora Lares sabía que el vestido costaba mil doscientos dólares antes de probárselo.   C   F

8. La señora Lares compra el vestido con su tarjeta de crédito.   C   F

Lección 7
El hogar y los muebles

Conversación ·

A. Listen to the dialogue as you read along. *Gabriela y Rodolfo Suárez, un joven matrimonio venezolano, está buscando casa.*

Gabriela:	Estoy cansada de buscar casa, mi amor. Yo creo que tenemos que decidirnos de una vez.
Rodolfo:	Estoy de acuerdo contigo, Gabriela. ¿Cuál de los apartamentos te gustó más?
Gabriela:	El condominio de la Urbanización Los Pinos. Es muy cómodo, me parece, y también necesita poco trabajo de remodelación.
Rodolfo:	Tienes razón. La sala es muy grande, y la cocina es moderna.
Gabriela:	Exactamente. La cocina tiene un refrigerador nuevo, estufa y lavaplatos.
Rodolfo:	Y tiene tres dormitorios. Yo quería un apartamento de tres dormitorios para usar el tercero como estudio.
Gabriela:	Y tiene una terraza muy grande con un panorama estupendo de la ciudad.
Rodolfo:	Otra cosa que tiene es que está cerca del metro. No voy a tener que manejar todos los días para llegar a la oficina.
Gabriela:	Tenemos que comprar muchos muebles: sofá, sillones, una cama para nosotros, camas para el segundo dormitorio, librerías para tu estudio, una mesa para la computadora.
Rodolfo:	Sí, pero primero tenemos que comprar el condominio. Mañana hablo con la oficina para hacer los trámites.
Gabriela:	¡Qué suerte que nos gustó el mismo apartamento a los dos!

Vocabulario

decidirse to make up one's mind
de una vez once and for all
estar de acuerdo con to agree with
la remodelación remodeling

la terraza balcony
el metro subway
el trámite step, transaction

B. Now listen to statements about the conversation between Gabriela and Rodolfo. Write **C (cierto)** if they are true and **F (falso)** if they are not.

1. _____ 3. _____ 5. _____ 7. _____ 9. _____

2. _____ 4. _____ 6. _____ 8. _____ 10. _____

C. **¡Ya!** Answer each of the speaker's questions by saying that the action was already done. Use the preterit in your answer and replace any direct object nouns with the corresponding pronouns. Listen to the model. The speaker will confirm the correct response.

MODELO•••➤ You hear: ¿Cuándo vas a escribir la carta?
You say: **Ya la escribí.**

1. _____ 2. _____ 3. _____ 4. _____ 5. _____ 6. _____

D. **No. Esa persona, no.** Answer each of the speaker's questions by saying that the person asked about didn't do the action. Listen to the model. The speaker will confirm the correct response.

MODELO • • • ➤   You hear: Yo trabajé. ¿Y Paula?

                 You say: **Paula no trabajó.**

1. _____   2. _____   3. _____   4. _____   5. _____   6. _____

E. Tanto como tú. Answer each of the speaker's questions by saying that the person asked about did as much as the other person. Use **tanto como.** Listen to the model. The speaker will confirm the correct response.

MODELO • • • ➤   You hear: Teresa trabajó mucho. ¿Y Carolina?

                 You say: **Carolina trabajó tanto como Teresa.**

1. _____   2. _____   3. _____   4. _____   5. _____   6. _____

La combinación de dos complementos . . . .

A. En la residencia. Students are busy getting settled in the dorm and asking each other questions about rooms and furniture. Answer each question affirmatively, using double object pronouns. Listen to the model. The speaker will confirm the correct response.

MODELO • • • ➤   You hear: Carolina te dio las llaves?

                 You say: **Sí, me las dio.**

1. _____   3. _____   5. _____   7. _____

2. _____   4. _____   6. _____   8. _____

Números . . . .

A. En la mueblería. Clara Meléndez is in a furniture store looking for things for her new home. Write the price of each item you hear about in numerals; don't spell out the figures.

1. Este sofá cuesta _____ dólares.

2. Estos sillones cuestan _____ dólares.

3. Esta lámpara cuesta _____ dólares.

4. Esta cama cuesta _____ dólares.

5. Esta cómoda cuesta _____ dólares.

6. Este espejo cuesta _____ dólares.

B. En el rastro (*flea market*). Miguel Osorio is a graduate student who has just rented an unfurnished apartment. He has gone to the flea market to buy some cheap furniture. He is bargaining with a woman who has some pieces of furniture to sell. Preview the true-false statements that follow and then listen to the conversation between Miguel and the seller. Mark the statments **Cierto** or **Falso** depending on the content of their conversation. You will hear the conversation twice.

1. Miguel ve un escritorio que le interesa.   C   F

2. La vendedora pide setecientos dólares por el escritorio.   C   F

3. La vendedora dice que ofrece un precio especial porque Miguel es estudiante.   C   F

4. Es un escritorio nuevo.   C   F

5. Miguel empieza ofreciendo cincuenta dólares.   C   F

6. El escritorio es de madera y es muy grande.   C   F

7. Cuando la vendedora sugiere *(suggests)* el precio de cien dólares, Miguel le ofrece setenta.   C   F

8. El precio final es de cien dólares.   C   F

9. Miguel acepta el precio final, pero solamente si el precio incluye una silla.   C   F

10. Miguel decide no comprar el escritorio.   C   F

Lección 8
De viaje

Conversación ....

A. Listen to the dialogue between Janet and the Mexican immigration officer and customs officer as you read along.

Inspector: Adelante. Buenas tardes, señorita. Sus documentos, por favor.
Janet: Aquí tiene Ud. mi pasaporte y visa de estudiante.
Inspector: ¿Su dirección en México?
Janet: En casa de los Sánchez, Avenida de Michoacán, 167.
Inspector: Bueno, pase Ud. a la aduana.
(a few seconds of the sound of people moving with their luggage from immigration to customs)
Aduanero: Buenas tardes. ¿Cuánto equipaje trae Ud.?
Janet: Dos maletas y mi bolsa.
Aduanero: ¿Y ese maletín?
Janet: Es mi computadora portátil.
Aduanero: Bien. Todo está en orden. ¿Quisiera abrir las maletas, por favor?
Janet: Sí, cómo no. Como Ud. puede ver, todo es para mi uso personal.
Aduanero: Muy bien. Cierre las maletas. Ud. puede pasar. El siguiente...

B. Now listen to some statements about the conversation. If a statement is true, put an *X* in the blank before **sí;** if it is false put an *X* before **no.**

1. _____ sí   _____ no

2. _____ sí   _____ no

3. _____ sí   _____ no

4. _____ sí   _____ no

5. _____ sí   _____ no

C. Now listen to Janet's discussion with the Mexican officials, repeating what you hear in the pauses provided.

El pretérito de los verbos irregulares. ....

A. Use the preterit of **ir** to explain that each of these people went to the airport. Follow the model. The speaker will confirm the correct response.

MODELO• • • ➤ You hear: ¿Dónde estaba José?
    You answer: **Fue al aeropuerto.**

1. .....   2. .....   3. .....   4. .....   5. .....

B. Use the preterit of **hacer** to answer these questions about whether people are ready for their trips. Answer in each case that they packed. Follow the model. The speaker will confirm the correct response.

MODELO• • • ➤ You hear: ¿Anita está lista para su viaje?
    You answer: **Sí, ayer hizo las maletas.**

1. .....   2. .....   3. .....   4. .....   5. .....

C. Use the preterit of **venir** to say that these people didn't see Carolina because they came late. Follow the model. The speaker will confirm the correct response.

MODELO ● ● ● ➤   You hear: ¿Juan no vio a Carolina?
                       You answer: **No, vino tarde.**

1. .....   **2.** .....   **3.** .....   **4.** .....   **5.** .....

D. Use the preterit of **tener** to say that these people did what they did because they had to do it. Follow the model. The speaker will confirm the correct response.

MODELO ● ● ● ➤   You hear: ¿Por qué lo hizo Juan?
                       You answer: **Tuvo que hacerlo.**

1. .....   **2.** .....   **3.** .....   **4.** .....   **5.** .....

Comparaciones de desigualdad . . . .

A. Alejandro is talking about traveling. Converse with him by forming comparatives using the cues you see. Follow the model. The speaker will confirm the correct response.

MODELO ● ● ● ➤   You hear: El tren es rápido.
                       You see: menos/el avión
                       You say: El tren es menos rápido que el avión.

1. más/el viaje en tren

2. más/mi maleta

3. menos/los boletos

4. menos/el carro

5. más/la estación de trenes

B. **Los amigos.** Bárbara is asking you about the people at school. In each case, use a comparative and superlative to tell her about the people she mentions. Follow the model. The speaker will confirm the correct response.

MODELO ● ● ● ➤   You hear: Marcos es alto. ¿Y Pedro?
                       You say: Pedro es más alto que Marcos. Pedro es el más alto.

1. .....   **2.** .....   **3.** .....   **4.** .....   **5.** .....

Comparaciones de igualdad . . . .

A. **Ni más ni menos.** Answer the speaker by saying that you have as many of each thing mentioned as she does. Follow the model. The speaker will confirm the correct response.

MODELO ● ● ● ➤   You hear: Ustedes tienen muchos boletos.
                       You say: Bueno, tenemos tantos boletos como Ud.

1. .....   **2.** .....   **3.** .....   **4.** .....   **5.** .....

Dictado parcial . . . .

A. Listen to the following passage about the Incas. Fill in the missing words based on what you hear. The passage will be read twice.

Cuando los españoles 1. _____ a Sudamérica, encontraron un continente donde

2. _____ muchos indígenas. Algunos de los pueblos indígenas 3. _____ civilizaciones muy avanzadas. Los incas 4. _____ el pueblo indígena 5. _____ avanzado.

Los incas tenían un imperio que se extendía por gran parte de la costa del Pacífico. La mayor parte de los

6. _____ modernos de Perú, Ecuador y Bolivia eran parte del imperio inca. La capital era Cuzco

y la 7. _____ de los incas era el quechua, idioma que todavía se habla en esas partes de Sudamérica. Los incas adoraban el sol y cultivaban diferentes variedades de papas. Los europeos no

8. _____ la papa antes de venir a Sudamérica. Los españoles 9. _____ la papa a Europa, donde 10. _____ a cultivarse y a convertirse en un elemento muy importante de la dieta europea.

Los incas 11. _____ buenos ingenieros. 12. _____ formidables carreteras, muchos puentes y templos. Machu Picchu, ciudad-fortaleza en los 13. _____ de los Andes, es uno de los 14. _____ ejemplos de la arquitectura de los incas.

Lección 9
En el hotel

Conversación ·

A. Listen to the dialogue as you read along. Carlos Lozano arrives at the Hotel Alameda in Guadalajara, Mexico. He goes up to the reception desk to ask for the room he reserved. Note the meanings for **quedar(se)**:

1. quedar *to be left*
Queda uno. *There's one left.*
quedarle (a uno) *to have something left over*
No me queda más remedio. *I don't have any choice.*

2. quedarse *to stay*
Me quedo aquí. *I stay here.*

Recepcionista:	Muy buenas tardes, señor. Bienvenido al Hotel Alameda. ¿En qué puedo servirle?
Sr. Lozano:	Soy Carlos Lozano. Hice una reservación para esta noche. Espero que mi habitación esté lista.
Recepcionista:	Un momento, por favor. Lozano, Lozano... Lo siento, pero no encuentro su nombre.
Sr. Lozano:	Es imposible que no tengan la reservación. Llamé la semana pasada para hacerla. Busque más, por favor.
Recepcionista:	Lo siento, pero su nombre no aparece en la lista de hoy. Espere un minuto. Voy a hablar con el gerente.
Sr. Lozano:	Quiero que esto se arregle *(is fixed)* rápido. Viajé mucho hoy y tengo que descansar.
Recepcionista:	Queda una sola habitación, en el quinto piso. ¿La quiere usted?
Sr. Lozano:	Por supuesto. No me queda más remedio. ¿Cuánto es?
Recepcionista:	Son ocho mil pesos por noche. La habitación tiene televisor, aire acondicionado, y dos teléfonos. Y el desayuno está incluido. Firme el registro, por favor, y déjeme ver su tarjeta de crédito.
Sr. Lozano:	Aquí tiene mi tarjeta. Présteme un bolígrafo, por favor.
Recepcionista:	Tome, señor.

B. **¿Cierto o falso?** Listen to these statements about Carlos Lozano's conversation with the reception desk clerk and indicate whether they are true or false. You will hear each statement twice.

1. C F   **3.** C F   **5.** C F   **7.** C F   **9.** C F

2. C F   **4.** C F   **6.** C F   **8.** C F   **10.** C F

Los mandatos ·

A. Answer the speaker with the appropriate **Ud.** or **Uds.** command. Follow the models. The speaker will confirm the correct response.

MODELO• • • ➤   You hear: No sé si debo salir.
You say: **¿Por qué no? Salga Ud.**
You hear: No sabemos si debemos salir.
You say: **¿Por qué no? Salgan Uds.**

1. .....   **3.** .....   **5.** .....   **7.** .....   **9.** .....

2. .....   **4.** .....   **6.** .....   **8.** .....   **10.** .....

B. Answer the speaker with the appropriate affirmative **Ud.** or **Uds.** command of the reflexive verb. Follow the models. The speaker will confirm the correct response.

MODELO• • • ➤   You hear: ¿Puedo sentarme?
                        You say: **Sí, cómo no. Siéntese Ud.**
                        You hear: ¿Podemos sentarnos?
                        You say: **Sí, cómo no. Siéntense Uds.**

1. .....   **2.** .....   **3.** .....   **4.** .....   **5.** .....   **6.** .....

C. Answer the speaker with the appropriate negative **Ud.** or **Uds.** command of the reflexive verb. Follow the models. The speaker will confirm the correct response.

MODELO• • • ➤   You hear: ¿Debo sentarme?
                        You say: **No, no se siente Ud.**
                        You hear: ¿Debemos sentarnos?
                        You say: **No, no se sienten Uds.**

1. .....   **2.** .....   **3.** .....   **4.** .....   **5.** .....   **6.** .....

El subjuntivo con deseos. . . . .

A. El viaje a Monterrey. María Luisa will make a few statements about her upcoming trip to the city of Monterrey, Mexico. If her statements contain a subjunctive verb, put an *X* in the subjunctive column; otherwise, put an *X* in the nonsubjunctive column.

         Subjunctive   **Nonsubjunctive**

1. _____   _____

2. _____   _____

3. _____   _____

4. _____   _____

5. _____   _____

6. _____   _____

B. Lo que tú debes hacer. The speaker consults with you on what he has to do. Use the cue you see to give him your opinion on the action. Decide in each case whether you need to use the subjunctive. Follow the model. The speaker will confirm the correct response.

MODELO• • • ➤   You hear: ¿Debo salir ahora?
                        You see: Es preciso...
                        You say: **Es preciso que salgas ahora.**

1. Es necesario que...

2. Quiero que...

3. No quiero que...

4. Me alegro de que...

5. Espero que...

6. Sé que...

7. Siento que...

8. Creo que...

El subjuntivo con dudas . . . .

A. **Hoy tenemos visita.** Luis and Julia Domínguez are expecting Julia's sister, Alicia, her husband Ramiro, and their children today. Mr. Domínguez asks his wife some questions about the visit. She answers him using the cues you will see. Follow the model. The speaker will confirm the correct response.

MODELO• • • ➤   You hear: ¿Vienen pronto?
    You see: Es posible...
    You say: **Es posible que vengan pronto.**

1. Dudo que...

2. No creo que...

3. Es posible que...

4. Creo que...

5. No es cierto que...

B. **En el hotel Villa Dudosa.** Carolina has some serious doubts about this hotel. She counters everything her friend says about it with a negative. Follow the model. The speaker will confirm the correct response.

MODELO• • • ➤   You hear: Creo que el hotel es bueno.
    You say: **No creo que el hotel sea bueno.**

1. .....   **2.** .....   **3.** .....   **4.** .....   **5.** .....

C. Marcos is traveling with a friend. He asks his friend questions about various aspects of their trip. Answer his questions as though you were his friend. Press the STOP button after hearing each question twice. This will give you time to say your answer and then jot it down in the space provided. The speaker will then give a possible answer for you to repeat. Listen to the model.

MODELO• • • ➤   You hear: ¿Cuándo quieres que haga la reservación?
    You say and write: Quiero que hagas la reservación ahora.
    You hear: Quiero que hagas la reservación mañana.
    You repeat: **Quiero que hagas la reservación mañana.**

1. _____

2. _____

3. _____

4. _____

5. _____

6. _____

7. _____

8. _____

Lección 10
Las diversiones

Conversación •••

A. Listen to the dialogue as you read along. *Maritza y René de la Cruz, un joven matrimonio de Madrid, hacen planes para el fin de semana.*

Maritza:	¿Qué tal si vamos al cine este fin de semana?
René:	¡Vale! Con tal que sea una película cómica y no trágica. Aquí tienes el periódico para que veas lo que ponen.
Maritza:	A ver... a ver... el sábado ponen una comedia nueva a las ocho y a las diez de la noche. ¿Qué función prefieres?
René:	Bueno, ¿por qué no vamos a la de las ocho? Así, cuando salgamos del cine, podremos cenar. ¿Qué te parece?
Maritza:	De acuerdo. Y... ¿quieres invitar a Sofi y a Marcos?
René:	Sí,... a menos que ellos ya tengan otro compromiso.
Maritza:	Entonces debes llamarles y, si van, diles que nos veremos en la taquilla media hora antes.
René:	Por lo menos. Tú sabes que Sofi casi siempre llega tarde.
Maritza:	¡Bah! No sólo Sofi sino Marcos también.
René:	Bueno... bueno. Todo depende...

B. **¿Cierto o falso?** Listen to these statements about Maritza and René de la Cruz's conversation and indicate whether they are true or false. You will hear each statement twice.

1. C F **3.** C F **5.** C F **7.** C F

2. C F **4.** C F **6.** C F **8.** C F

El futuro •••

A. **No sé si esto pasará.** Answer the speaker saying that you don't know if these things will happen. Use the future tense in your answers. Follow the model. The speaker will confirm the correct response.

MODELO•••➤ You hear: ¿Se van José y Dora?
                You say: No sé si se irán.

1. .....   **2.** .....   **3.** .....   **4.** .....   **5.** .....   **6.** .....

B. **Mañana.** Say that the following things will happen tomorrow, not today as the speaker thinks. Use the future tense in your answers. Follow the model. The speaker will confirm the correct response.

MODELO•••➤ You hear: José y Dora se van hoy, ¿verdad?
                You say: No, se irán mañana.

1. .....   **2.** .....   **3.** .....   **4.** .....   **5.** .....   **6.** .....

El subjuntivo con algunas expresiones adverbiales •••••••••

A. Repeat the sentences you will hear. Then, say them again, using the adverbial conjunctions and subjects you hear. Follow the model. The speaker will confirm the correct response.

	You repeat:	Iremos al cine con tal de tener tiempo.
	You hear:	con tal que tú
	You say:	Iremos al cine con tal que tú tengas tiempo.
	You hear:	con tal que ustedes
	You say:	Iremos al cine con tal que ustedes tengan tiempo.

1. Sacaré las entradas para ver la película.

    a. .....

    b. .....

    c. .....

2. No me voy de aquí antes de hablar con el profesor.

    a. .....

    b. .....

    c. .....

3. Nadie sale sin querer.

    a. .....

    b. .....

    c. .....

4. Nos veremos con tal de llegar por la mañana.

    a. .....

    b. .....

    c. .....

5. Terminaré el trabajo para poder salir.

    a. .....

    b. .....

    c. .....

6. No lo vamos a hacer sin tener el permiso de papá.

    a. .....

    b. .....

    c. .....

7. Vamos a cenar antes de ir al concierto.

a. .....

b. .....

c. .....

8. Iremos con tal de no estar muy ocupados.

a. .....

b. .....

c. .....

El subjuntivo con otras expresiones adverbiales. . . . .

A. Cuando pueda. Answer each of the following questions saying that people will do this thing when they can. Follow the model. The speaker will confirm the correct response.

MODELO • • • ➤ You hear: ¿Cuándo lo van a hacer los muchachos?
You answer: Lo harán cuando puedan.

1. ..... **2.** ..... **3.** ..... **4.** ..... **5.** ..... **6.** .....

B. Cuando haya tiempo. Repeat each sentence after the speaker. Then, when you hear the cue **Cambie,** change the first verb from present to future and make all necessary changes. Follow the model. The speaker will confirm the correct response.

MODELO • • • ➤ You hear: Salimos cuando tenemos tiempo.
You repeat: Salimos cuando tenemos tiempo.
You hear: Cambie.
You say: Saldremos cuando tengamos tiempo.

1. ..... **2.** ..... **3.** ..... **4.** ..... **5.** ..... **6.** .....

Las preposiciones *para* y *por*. . . . .

A. Listen to what the speaker says. Then circle the letter of the sentence that responds to it logically. Follow the model. You will hear each statement twice.

MODELO • • • ➤ You hear: Las entradas costaron mucho dinero, ¿verdad?
You see: a. Sí, pagué cien dólares para ellos.
b. Sí, pagué cien dólares por ellos.
The correct answer is b.

1. a. Es por ti.
  b. Es para ti.

2. a. No, para el viernes.
  b. No, por el viernes.

3. a. Sí, mucho. Estudio para ser enfermera.
  b. Sí, mucho. Estudio por ser enfermera.

4. a. Sí, para eso.
   b. Sí, por eso.

5. a. Sí, me la puse por ella.
   b. Sí, me la puse para ella.

Los pronombres con preposiciones. . . . .

A. **Personas necesarias.** Your friend asks you which of two people you need. Answer in each case that you need the first one, using the appropriate pronoun after the preposition. Follow the model. The speaker will confirm the correct response.

   MODELO • • • ➤   You hear: ¿Necesitas a Marcos y a Claudia?
                       You say: A él, sí. A ella, no.

   1. .....   **2.** .....   **3.** .....   **4.** .....   **5.** .....   **6.** .....

B. **Gustos.** Your friend asks you which of two people likes certain things. Answer in each case that the second person mentioned likes them, using the appropriate pronoun after the preposition. Follow the model. The speaker will confirm the correct response.

   MODELO • • • ➤   You hear: ¿A quién le gusta el helado de chocolate? ¿A Juan o a Laura?
                       You say: A él, no. A ella, sí.

   1. .....   **2.** .....   **3.** .....   **4.** .....   **5.** .....   **6.** .....

Dictado. . . . .

A. **Arte y arquitectura en el mundo hispano.** Listen twice to this section on art and architecture in the Spanish-speaking world. Take notes on what you hear. Then you will hear a series of descriptions. Write the number of each description next to the person or place it describes.
Vocabulario
una catedral gótica a Gothic cathedral
los restos remains

_____

_____

_____

_____

_____

_____

_____

_____

_____

_____

_____

_____

_____

_____

_____

_____

_____

_____

_____

_____

_____

B. Now write the numbers of the descriptions next to the person or place they refer to.

_____ **Sevilla**

_____ **Frida Kahlo**

_____ **El Escorial**

_____ **Quito**

_____ **Cuzco**

_____ **San Juan de Teotihuacán**

_____ **Velázquez**

Answer Key
to the Workbook

Lección preliminar

¡Saludos!

Conversación . . . .

A. Fill in the missing words. This dialogue is in the **tú** form.

Fernando: Hola, Miguel. Buenas <u>tardes</u>.
Miguel: <u>Buenas</u> tardes, Fernando. ¿<u>Qué</u> tal?
Fernando: Bien, <u>gracias</u>. ¿Cómo <u>estás</u> tú?
Miguel: Más o <u>menos</u>.
Fernando: Huy, <u>es</u> tarde. Perdón.
Miguel: <u>Hasta</u> luego, Fernando.

B. Fill in the missing words. This dialogue is in the **Ud.** form.

Señora Ochoa: Buenos <u>días</u>, señorita Soto.
Señorita Soto: Ah, <u>señora</u> Ochoa. ¿Cómo <u>está</u> Ud.?
Señora Ochoa: <u>Estoy</u> bastante bien, gracias. ¿ <u>Y</u> Ud.?
Señorita Soto: Yo estoy <u>bien</u>.
Señora Ochoa: Perdón, señorita. Es <u>tarde</u>. Adiós.
Señorita Soto: Ah, sí. Adiós, señora.

Cultura . . . .

A. **1.** ciudades　　**2.** hispanos　　**3.** países　　**4.** mexicano　　**5.** la Florida　　**6.** las palabras

Alfabeto . . . .

A. **1.** f　　**2.** j　　**3.** k　　**4.** ñ　　**5.** y　　**6.** v　　**7.** ll　　**8.** z　　**9.** h　　**10.** w
B. **1.** ache - u - ge - o　　**2.** ele - a - u - ere - a　　**3.** pe - a - be - ele - o　　**4.** uve - e - ere - a
5. i griega - o - ele - a - ene - de - a

Números 0–99 . . . .

A. **1.** cincuenta y nueve pesos　　**2.** veintidós pesos　　**3.** ochenta y cuatro pesos　　**4.** sesenta y siete pesos
5. dieciocho pesos　　**6.** trece pesos　　**7.** treinta y seis pesos　　**8.** cuarenta y cinco pesos
9. setenta y ocho pesos　　**10.** noventa pesos

Expresiones para la clase . . . .

A. **1.** abrir　　**2.** cerrar　　**3.** Cuál　　**4.** una ciudad

¿Cómo se dice? . . . .

A. **1.** leer/el correo electrónico　　**2.** Es　　**3.** Vamos a　　**4.** hablan

Orígenes . . . .

A. **1.** puertorriqueña　　**2.** norteamericano　　**3.** cubano　　**4.** norteamericana　　**5.** mexicano
6. cubana

Vamos a leer (y a escribir) . . . .

A. **1.** $14.99—catorce noventa y nueve; $15.99—quince noventa y nueve; $19.99—diecinueve noventa y nueve.
2. cinco-cincuenta y ocho-dieciséis-veintitrés.

Lección I

La clase y las presentaciones

Conversación. . . . .

A. En la clase.

José Luis: Buenos días. <u>¿Cómo</u> te llamas?

Felisa: <u>Me llamo</u> Felisa Camacho. ¿Y <u>tú</u>?

José Luis: Me llamo <u>José Luis</u> Peña.

Felisa: Mucho <u>gusto</u>, José Luis.

José Luis: El <u>gusto</u> es <u>mío</u>, Felisa.

B. En la oficina.

Marcos Lares: Buenos días. <u>Me</u> llamo Marcos Lares. <u>Soy</u> ingeniero. ¿Cómo <u>se</u> <u>llama</u> Ud., señorita?

Elena Soto: Buenos días. Yo <u>me</u> <u>llamo</u> Elena Soto. <u>Soy</u> programadora.

Marcos Lares: <u>Encantado</u>, señorita.

Elena Soto: <u>Encantada</u>.

Sujetos. . . . .

A. Tú vs. Ud. **1.** ¿De dónde eres? **2.** ¿De dónde es Ud.? **3.** ¿De dónde es Ud.?
4. ¿De dónde eres? **5.** ¿De dónde es Ud.?

Pronombres. . . . .

A. **1.** yo **2.** ella **3.** él **4.** ellas **5.** nosotros

B. Pronombres. **1.** ¿<u>Tú</u> eres de Colombia? ¡<u>Yo</u> soy de Colombia también! **2.** José y Teresa Lara son profesores. <u>Él</u> es profesor de español y <u>ella</u> es profesora de inglés. **3.** —¿De dónde son Rafael y Pedro? ¿De Venezuela? —No, de Venezuela no. <u>Ellos</u> son de Guatemala. Amalia y Laura son de Venezuela. **4.** —Luis y Tomás, ¿<u>Uds. (Ustedes)</u> son ingenieros? <u>Nosotras</u> somos ingenieras también.

El verbo *ser*. . . . .

A. ¿Qué son y de dónde son? **1.** Yo soy estudiante. Soy de los Estados Unidos. **2.** La señora Morales es profesora. Es de Venezuela. **3.** Carlos y yo somos actores. Somos de España. **4.** Tú eres escritor. Eres de Cuba. **5.** Ustedes son licenciados. Son de Puerto Rico. **6.** Mauricio es cantante. Es de México. **7.** Usted es abogada. Es de Guatemala. **8.** Rosa y Pedro son directores. Son de Chile.

En el salón de clase. . . . .

A. **1.** la mochila **2.** la silla **3.** el lápiz **4.** la calculadora **5.** los estudiantes
6. la luz **7.** la pizarra **8.** los libros

Sustantivos y artículos . . . .

A. La escuela de Juanito. **1.** un **2.** unas **3.** unos **4.** unas **5.** un **6.** una

B. Me gusta(n). **1.** Me gustan/No me gustan las **2.** Me gusta/No me gusta el **3.** Me gusta/No me gusta la **4.** Me gustan/No me gustan las **5.** Me gustan/No me gustan los **6.** Me gusta/No me gusta el **7.** Me gusta/No me gusta el **8.** Me gustan/No me gustan los

C. Gustos. **1.** —¿Te gustan las lecciones? —Sí, me gustan. **2.** —¿Te gusta el reloj? —No, no me gusta. **3.** —¿Te gustan los cantantes? —No, no me gustan. **4.** —¿Te gusta el baloncesto? —Sí, me gusta. **5.** —¿Te gusta la computadora? —No, no me gusta.

Vamos a leer . . . .

A. **1.** Tae Kwon Do and Karate **2.** No, there is a picture of a child. **3.** There is a square surrounded by a dotted line that looks like a coupon. **4.** The instructor is from Korea: **instructor koreano** **5.** The word for children is **niños: Clases para adultos y niños.** **6.** coupon: cupón; free: **gratis**

7. discipline: **disciplina**   respect: **respeto**   excellence: **excelencia**   self-confidence: **autoconfianza**   **8.** One free session: **1 sesión gratis con este cupón**

Vamos a escribir . . . .

Composition exercise.

Lección 2

La familia y las descripciones

A. **La familia de Javier Rojo.**   **1.** llamo   **2.** Soy   **3.** Estudio   **4.** clases   **5.** gusta
6. hablar   **7.** somos   **8.** es   **9.** la universidad   **10.** interesantes
B. **Mi familia y yo.** *Composition exercise.*
C. **La familia de Pablito Ortega.**   Fill in the blanks within the illustration with the appropriate term: los abuelos, los padres, la hermana, las primas, el tío, la tía, la madre, la abuela, and el abuelo.

Las descripciones . . . .

A. **Mis asociaciones.** *Answers will vary.*
B. **Busco novio(a).** *Composition exercise.*

El presente de los verbos regulares en-*ar* . . . .

A. **1.** trabaja   **2.** enseña   **3.** necesitas   **4.** visitan   **5.** escuchamos   **6.** tomo
B. **Mi día.** The verb forms: **estudio, desayuno, descanso, escucho, camino, preparo, regreso, miro**

El verbo *estar* . . . .

A. **¿Cómo están y dónde están?**   **1.** Yo estoy cansada. Estoy en el gimnasio.   **2.** Marcos y Francisco están entusiasmados. Están aquí.   **3.** Alfredo y yo estamos ocupados. Estamos en la oficina.   **4.** Marta y Raquel están calladas. Están en la clase.   **5.** Tú estás aburrida. Estás en la biblioteca.
B. **Los gemelos.**   **1.** son/Son   **2.** Son   **3.** son/Son   **4.** están   **5.** son/están
6. están/son   **7.** está/están   **8.** están   **9.** Están   **10.** es/están

Vamos a leer . . . .

A. **1.** a technical school   **2.** English   **3.** Higher education: **educación superior;** graduate studies: **postgrados**   **4. Politécnico Colombo Andino.** The Andes mountains: **andino.**   **5.** Bilingual executive secretary, translator, technical translator; translation = **traducción**   **6.** Systems engineering: **ingeniería de sistemas**   **7.** system analysis and design, business administration, bilingual executive secretary, English translation; by day: **diurno** by night: **nocturno**   **8a. administración de empresas**   **8b. análisis y diseño de sistemas**   **8c.** accountants: **especialización en informática para contadores**

Lección 3

Las comidas

Conversación. . . . .

A. **1.** Estados Unidos   **2.** estudia (está *also possible*)   **3.** restaurante   **4.** preparan
5. deliciosos   **6.** tortilla   **7.** queso   **8.** comer   **9.** mesero   **10.** guapo

Cultura

A. **1.** el pescado **2.** la paella **3.** comemos **4.** tacos **5.** picante **6.** carne **7.** frutas

Ir

A. **1.** ¿Adónde va Felipe? Va al cine. **2.** ¿Adónde van los García? Van al mercado. **3.** ¿Adónde va Rosario? Va al restaurante. **4.** ¿Adónde voy? Vas a la universidad. **5.** ¿Adónde van ustedes? Vamos a la ciudad. **6.** ¿Adónde va el mesero? Va a la mesa.

Ir a + *infinitive*

A. **Planes.** Answers will vary.

El presente de los verbos -*er/-ir*

A. **¿Qué hacen?** **1.** escribo **2.** debes **3.** ve **4.** abrimos **5.** comparten **6.** leo **7.** aprendes **8.** comemos

Las preguntas

A. **1.** ¿Llegan los estudiantes temprano? **2.** ¿Enseña cada profesor cinco clases? **3.** ¿Leen los estudiantes muchos libros? **4.** ¿Enseña la profesora Jiménez español?
B. **1.** ¿Dónde estudian tus amigos? **2.** ¿Quién enseña biología? **3.** ¿Adónde vas mañana? **4.** ¿De dónde es Isabel Morales?

La *a* personal

A. **1.** a **2.** — **3.** a **4.** a **5.** — **6.** a

Saber y *conocer*

A. **Preguntas.** **1.** ¿Sabes el vocabulario? **2.** ¿Sabes cocinar? **3.** ¿Conoces a la hermana de Mario? **4.** ¿Conoces el nuevo restaurante mexicano? **5.** ¿Sabes qué son chilaquiles? **6.** ¿Sabes de dónde es Lola Laredo? **7.** ¿Conoces Puerto Rico? **8.** ¿Sabes que José vive aquí?

El tiempo

A. *(possible answers)* **1.** Hace (mucho) calor y hace sol. **2.** Llueve (mucho) y hace frío. **3.** Hace mucho frío y mucho viento. Nieva mucho. **4.** Hace buen tiempo. No hace mucho calor.

Vamos a leer

A. **1.** Nutrition experts **(expertos en nutrición)** **2.** They see no problems with it. **(no ven problemas)** **3.** vegetables **4.** **seis cebollas grandes** **5.** **medio kilo de tomates** **6.** pepper: **pimiento;** a pinch: **una pizca;** celery: **apio;** chicken broth: **caldo de pollo** **7.** Cut the vegetables into small- or medium-sized pieces, boil them, and put them through a blender. **8.** Either cold or hot **(fría o caliente).**

Lección 4

Las actividades diarias

Horario

A. **Una estudiante universitaria.** **1.** F. Rafaela almuerza a las doce los lunes, los miércoles y los viernes. Los martes y los jueves almuerza a la una. **2.** T **3.** T **4.** F. Los lunes y los miércoles Rafaela va al laboratorio de lenguas. Va al laboratorio de física los viernes. **5.** F. Rafaela tiene clase de administración de empresas dos veces por semana: los lunes y los miércoles.   **6.** C   **7.** F. Rafaela tiene clase de gimnasia los lunes y los miércoles.   **8.** C

Cultura . . . .

(answers may vary slightly)

A. **1.** ...los estudiantes asisten a un año de preparatoria antes de entrar en la universidad.   **2.** ...no tienen opciones. Sus programas son rígidos.   **3.** ...es aparte de la universidad.   **4.** ...no tienen residencias.   **5.** ...no hay equipos deportivos.

Los adjetivos posesivos . . . .

A. **1.** Nuestra clase es interesante.   **2.** Mis tareas son difíciles.   **3.** Nuestros amigos son simpáticos.   **4.** Tus reuniones son importantes.   **5.** Aquí está su horario, señor.

B. **La posesión.**
1. El reloj es del profesor.   **2.** El bolígrafo es del chico mexicano.   **3.** Los lápices son de la amiga de Pedro.   **4.** Los cuadernos son de los nuevos estudiantes.   **5.** El papel es del muchacho español.

Actividades . . . .

A. Mario cierra la puerta. Mario empieza la lección. Mario puede estudiar química. Mario entiende el manual.
Tú: Almuerzas en la universidad. Empiezas la lección. Vuelves a casa. Los estudiantes cierran la puerta. Los estudiantes almuerzan en la universidad. Los estudiantes entienden el manual.
Yo: Almuerzo en la universidad. Empiezo la lección. Entiendo el manual. Vuelvo a casa. Mis amigos y yo cerramos la puerta. Mis amigos y yo empezamos la lección. Mis amigos y yo volvemos a casa.

Verbos con cambios en el presente . . . .

A. **Yo también.**   **1.** viene/vengo   **2.** sale/salgo   **3.** hacen/hago   **4.** traen/traigo
5. pones/pongo

Los pronombres reflexivos . . . .

A. **Un día típico.**   **1.** me despierto   **2.** me quedo   **3.** Me levanto   **4.** Me ducho
5. me pongo   **6.** me voy   **7.** asisto   **8.** me divierto   **9.** me pongo   **10.** me acuesto

B. **El día típico de Andrés.**   **1.** se despierta   **2.** se queda   **3.** Se levanta   **4.** Se ducha
5. se pone   **6.** se va   **7.** asiste   **8.** se divierte   **9.** se pone   **10.** se acuesta

La hora . . . .

A. **¿Qué hora es?**   **1.** Son las tres de la tarde.   **2.** Son las doce y veinticinco de la noche.   **3.** Son las ocho menos diez de la mañana.   **4.** Son las nueve y cuarto de la noche.   **5.** Es la una y media de la tarde.

B. **¿A qué hora?**   **1.** Salen cinco aviones.   **2.** El primer avión sale a las seis de la mañana los martes.   **3.** El último avión sale a las veintitrés horas (a las once de la noche) los jueves.   **4.** El segundo avión sale a las trece horas (a la una de la tarde) los domingos.   **5.** El último avión sale a las diecinueve horas (a las siete de la tarde) los domingos.

Vamos a leer . . . .

A. **1.** **Universidad Adolfo Ibáñez**   **2.** **Viña del Mar** and **Santiago**   **3.** **Postulación**   **4.** Students in search of academic excellence.   **5.** Commercial engineering (**Ingeniería Comercial**)   **6.** law: **derecho;** journalism: **periodismo**   **7.** **Pedagogía en Enseñanza Media**   **8.** January 9, 1998.
9. No preparation necessary (**no requiere preparación previa**)

Lección 5

La salud y el cuerpo

El cuerpo humano . . . .

A. **1.** la espalda   **2.** el pecho   **3.** el estómago   **4.** el pie   **5.** la pierna   **6.** la rodilla   **7.** los dedos del pie   **8.** la mano   **9.** los dedos   **10.** el brazo   **11.** la cabeza   **12.** el hombro   **13.** el codo   **14.** los ojos   **15.** la nariz   **16.** la boca   **17.** los dientes   **18.** los labios   **19.** la cara   **20.** la oreja   **21.** el corazón   **22.** el cerebro   **23.** la sangre   **24.** el oído   **25.** la garganta   **26.** el hueso   **27.** el riñón   **28.** los pulmones

B. **1.** b   **2.** c   **3.** a   **4.** c   **5.** c

Verbos con cambio en el presente . . . .

A. **1.** pides; Pido vitaminas/aspirinas.   **2.** pide; Pide una receta/una dieta.   **3.** piden; Pedimos antibióti-cos/una inyección.

B. **1.** pregunta   **2.** pregunto   **3.** pedir   **4.** pide   **5.** pregunto

Expresiones con *tener* . . . .

A. **1.** tengo (mucha) hambre   **2.** tiene (mucha) prisa   **3.** Tienes razón   **4.** tienen (mucho) frío   **5.** Tenemos sed   **6.** tenemos (mucho) calor   **7.** Tengo (mucho) miedo   **8.** tengo   **9.** Tengo ganas   **10.** Tienes que

El presente progresivo . . . .

A. **¡Gripe en la residencia!**   **1.** Tomás y Pedro están llamando al médico.   **2.** Paula y yo nos estamos preparando (estamos preparándonos) un té caliente.   **3.** Alfredo está durmiendo.   **4.** Yo estoy descansando.   **5.** Tú estás tomando antibióticos.

Los pronombres de complemento directo . . . .

A. **1.** las pido   **2.** lo sirve   **3.** la cerramos   **4.** te ayudo   **5.** me recuerda   **6.** los cocino

B. **Conversaciones.**   **1.** ¿Tienen Uds. que seguir la dieta? No, no la tenemos que seguir. *or* No, no tenemos que seguirla.   **2.** ¿Vas a comer muchos vegetales? Sí, los voy a comer. *or* Sí, voy a comerlos.   **3.** ¿Debo evitar el estrés? Sí, lo debe(s) evitar. *or* Sí, debe(s) evitarlo.   **4.** ¿Puede Ud. tomar esta medicina? No, no la puedo tomar. *or* No, no puedo tomarla.   **5.** ¿Quieres ver al médico? No, no lo quiero ver. *or* No, no quiero verlo.   **6.** ¿Debemos pedir la misma receta? Sí, la debemos pedir. *or* Sí, debemos pedirla.

Vamos a leer . . . .

A. **1.** dentistry and podiatry; **dientes, dental; pies**   **2.** Around Christmas; **Feliz Navidad** means *Merry Christmas.*   **3.** The foot clinic. **Consultas** means *medical visits.*   **4.** toothache: **dolor de muelas;** ath-lete's foot: **pie de atleta;** treatment: **(el) tratamiento;** cosmetic dentistry: **odontología cosmética**
5a. bleeding gums (**¿Sangran sus encías?**)   **5b.** tooth decay (**caries**), missing teeth (**¿Faltan dientes?**), toothache (**¿Dolor de muelas?**), broken or spotted teeth (**¿Dientes quebrados y/o manchados?**)
5c. hangnails   **5d.** dental clinic: **mal aliento**—bad breath; foot clinic: **mal olor** bad smell   **5e.** Smile confidently (=without complexes).

B. **La vida de un joven médico.**   **1.** a   **2.** c   **3.** b   **4.** a   **5.** b

Lección 6

En la tienda de ropa

La ropa . . . .

A. **¿Cómo es esta ropa?**   **1.** La falda negra es de lana.   **2.** Los calcetines marrón (marrones) son de nilón.   **3.** La corbata amarilla es de seda.   **4.** La blusa blanca es de algodón.   **5.** Los pantalones grises son de poliéster. *or* El pantalón gris es de poliéster.

B. **¿Qué ropa ponerse?** *Answers will vary.*

Los adjetivos y los pronombres demostrativos . . . .

A. **¡Tantos hijos!**   **1.** ¿Esos zapatos? No, mamá. Quiero ponerme aquéllos.   **2.** ¿Esos pantalones? No, mamá. Quiero ponerme aquéllos.   **3.** ¿Ese vestido? No, mamá. Quiero ponerme aquél.   **4.** ¿Esa camisa? No, mamá. Quiero ponerme aquélla.   **5.** ¿Esas botas? No, mamá. Quiero ponerme aquéllas.   **6.** ¿Esa sudadera? No, mamá. Quiero ponerme aquélla.

B. **En la tienda de ropa.**   **1.** No, ésa no me gusta. Aquella falda me gusta más.   **2.** No, ése no me gusta. Aquel paraguas me gusta más.   **3.** No, ésas no me gustan. Aquellas cadenas de oro me gustan más.   **4.** No, ésos no me gustan. Aquellos aretes me gustan más.   **5.** No, ése no me gusta. Aquel suéter me gusta más.   **6.** No, ésas no me gustan. Aquellas sandalias me gustan más.

El imperfecto del pasado . . . .

A. **Recuerdos.**   **1.** era   **2.** Compraba   **3.** sabía   **4.** Llevaba   **5.** usaba   **6.** salía   **7.** se ponía   **8.** llevaba   **9.** admirábamos   **10.** queríamos

B. **Cuando yo era niño(a)...** *Answers will vary.*

Los pronombres de complemento indirecto . . . .

A. **¿A quién?**   **1.** Sí, les mandé las invitaciones a todos mis amigos.   **2.** Sí, le regalé la pulsera a mi novia.   **3.** Sí, Juan me prestó sus casetes a mí.   **4.** Sí, le escribimos la carta a Carlos Pérez.   **5.** Sí, el profesor les dijo las respuestas a los estudiantes.   **6.** Sí, te compramos un regalo a ti.

B. **Hay que ayudar a la gente.**   **1.** Sí. ¿Por qué no les prestamos estas corbatas a los chicos?   **2.** Sí. ¿Por qué no le devolvemos su paraguas a Marcos?   **3.** Sí. ¿Por qué no le regalamos una sudadera roja a Carolina?   **4.** Sí. ¿Por qué no le compramos una gorra de lana a Pablito?   **5.** Sí. ¿Por qué no les decimos la dirección de la tienda a Matilde y Julia?   **6.** Sí. ¿Por qué no les enseñamos el catálogo a Sergio y Andrés?

Los pronombres indirectos con *gustar* y verbos similares. . . . .

A. **Opiniones y reacciones.**   **1.** Me gustan los hoteles, pero no me gusta la comida.   **2.** Le interesa la historia, pero no le interesan las ciencias.   **3.** Me duelen los oídos, pero no me duele la garganta.   **4.** Nos encanta el fútbol, pero no nos encanta la natación.   **5.** Las blusas me parecen lindas, pero el vestido me parece feo.   **6.** Les gusta el teatro, pero no les gustan los partidos.

B. **La moda de hoy.** *Composition exercise.*

Vamos a leer . . . .

A.   **1.** The end of the year and the coming new year. (**Para celebrar el fin de año...**)   **2.** Until December 31 (**Hasta el 31 de diciembre.**)   **3.** **Regalo.**   **4.** The stores are open either from 11 to 9 or from 10 to 10 on Sundays.   **5a-d.** *Answers will vary.*

Lección 7

El hogar y los muebles

El hogar y los muebles . . . .

A. 1. F 2. F 3. C 4. F 5. C 6. C 7. F 8. F 9. F 10. C

El pretérito de los verbos en -*ar* . . . .

A. 1. alquilé 2. Empecé 3. me levanté 4. compré 5. miré 6. busqué 7. encontré 8. Hablé 9. recomendó 10. Llamé 11. enseñaron 12. gustó 13. Me mudé 14. ayudaron 15. invité 16. trabajamos 17. pasamos 18. terminamos

El pretérito de los verbos en -*er* e -*ir* . . . .

A. Fue ayer. 1. Sí, comí tacos ayer. 2. Sí, recibí correo electrónico ayer. 3. Sí, corrí ayer. 4. Sí, oí música ayer. 5. Sí, salí con los amigos ayer. 6. Sí, leí el periódico ayer. 7. Sí, asistí al concierto ayer. 8. Sí, fui a la biblioteca ayer.

B. Entre amigos. 1. Marta fue a la universidad. 2. José durmió toda la mañana. 3. Sara y Marcos repitieron el nuevo vocabulario. 4. Luis le pidió ayuda al profesor de química. 5. La cafetería sirvió comida mexicana. 6. Los estudiantes se divirtieron comiendo tacos y enchiladas. 7. Carolina prefirió comer en casa. 8. Ella no se divirtió. 9. Lola leyó cien páginas. 10. Yo leí doscientas páginas.

La combinación de dos complementos. . . . .

A. Mala memoria. 1. ¿No te acuerdas? Ya te la enseñé. 2. ¿No te acuerdas? Ya te lo devolví. 3. ¿No te acuerdas? Ya te la regalé. 4. ¿No te acuerdas? Ya te las di. 5. ¿No te acuerdas? Ya te los vendí. 6. ¿No te acuerdas? Ya te lo alquilé.

B. Ya lo hicimos. 1. Ya se los dimos. 2. Ya se lo buscamos. 3. Ya se los sacamos. 4. Ya se las limpiamos. 5. Ya se las pedimos. 6. Ya se lo servimos.

Los números 100–1000+ . . . .

A. Comprando muebles. 1. sofá/quinientos noventa dólares 2. alfombra/novecientos cuarenta y ocho dólares 3. lámpara/ciento dos dólares 4. cama/cuatrocientos treinta y nueve dólares 5. lavadora secadora/setecientos ochenta y nueve dólares

Vamos a leer . . . .

A. 1. terraza 2. hab.=habitaciones; mts.=metros 3. **quinta** 4. three levels; **el nivel** 5. **la quinta** 6. **Town House; vigilancia** 7. **Quinta:** 4; **Town House:** 3 8. Large green space: 10.000.000 mts. de áreas verdes

Lección 8

De viaje

A. 1. i 2. f 3. a 4. h 5. c 6. b 7. j 8. d 9. g 10. e

B. La señora Arias hizo un viaje. 1. fue al aeropuerto en taxi 2. llegó al aeropuerto 3. tuvo que hacer cola 4. se acercó al mostrador 5. saludó al agente 6. enseñó su boleto 7. recibió su tarjeta de embarque 8. fue a la puerta para abordar

C. ¿Temprano o tarde? 1. puerta 2. quince 3. temprano 4. atención 5. puntual 6. tarde 7. reloj 8. restaurante 9. novela 10. avión/vuelo 11. asiento 12. otro

El pretérito de los verbos irregulares...

A. **1.** hicieron   **2.** fui   **3.** Hizo   **4.** Fuimos   **5.** pudimos

B. **1.** me desperté   **2.** pude   **3.** tuve   **4.** dije   **5.** dio   **6.** trajo   **7.** me quedé   **8.** me
sentí   **9.** fui

C. **Ya lo hicieron**   **1.** Ya me la dijeron.   **2.** Ya lo puse allí.   **3.** Ya nos los dio. *or* Ya se los dio.
4. Ya la hizo   **5.** Ya vino.   **6.** Ya lo hizo

Contrastes entre el imperfecto y el pretérito..

A. **¿Imperfecto o pretérito?**   **1.** nació   **2.** Era   **3.** gustaban   **4.** era   **5.** no quería
6. Se hizo   **7.** Consiguió   **8.** conoció   **9.** tenían   **10.** se enamoraron/se casaron
11. decidió/quería   **12.** empezaron

B. **Una carta.**   **1.** fue   **2.** salió   **3.** llegó   **4.** eran   **5.** había   **6.** conocí   **7.** sirvieron
8. conversábamos   **9.** leían   **10.** jugaban   **11.** pasaron   **12.** decidí   **13.** quería
14. dormía   **15.** estaba   **16.** pude   **17.** pasé   **18.** aterrizó   **19.** bajamos   **20.** fuimos
21. pasé   **22.** hicieron   **23.** busqué   **24.** llegué   **25.** eran   **26.** quería   **27.** estaba
28. pude   **29.** me acosté   **30.** dormí

C. *Composition exercise.*

Las comparaciones de desigualdad...

A. **1.** El viaje a Buenos Aires es más largo que el viaje a París. Es menos fácil que el viaje a París.   **2.** Brasil
es más grande que Honduras. Es más caro que Honduras.   **3.** En Panamá hace más calor que en Chile.
Hace menos fresco que en Chile.   **4.** La comida vegetariana es más sabrosa que esta comida. Es mejor
que esta comida.   **5.** El avión es más rápido que el tren. Es mejor que el tren.   **6.** Esta ciudad es más
ruidosa que la capital. Es peor que la capital.

Las comparaciones de igualdad...

A. **Gente afín.**   **1.** Margarita es tan generosa como Isabel.   **2.** Samuel es tan inteligente como Marisa.
3. Carolina es tan buena como Bárbara.   **4.** Amalia es tan estudiosa como Pedro.   **5.** Víctor es tan
amante de los deportes como Manuel.

B. **Muchos viajes.**   **1.** tantos comprobantes como yo   **2.** tantas tarjetas de embarque como yo
3. tantas maletas como yo   **4.** tantos pasajes como yo   **5.** tanto equipaje como yo   **6.** tantos vuelos como yo

Vamos a leer...

A. **1.** A round trip to New York by plane.   **2.** From Madrid or Málaga to New York.   **3.** Prices of two
different packages.   **4.** Una vez por semana, los jueves.   **5.** Siete noches de hotel.   **6.** Hay que pagar un suplemento.   **7.** Es grande. Tiene 250 oficinas.   **8.** Las plazas están limitadas.

Lección 9

En el hotel

A. **1.** i   **2.** c   **3.** b   **4.** a   **5.** h   **6.** j   **7.** f   **8.** d   **9.** g   **10.** e   **11.** k   **12.** l

Vamos a leer...

A. **1.** Hotel Victoria   **2.** Oaxaca   **3.** Tres: Estándar, Villa, Junior Suite   **4.** Queda a cuatro horas y
media de México.   **5.** El tenis (el anuncio menciona que hay cancha de tenis).   **6.** Incluye el desayuno y la estancia de dos niños menores de catorce años gratis, no incluye impuestos ni propinas.
7. Un quince por ciento de descuento en comidas y cenas, un quince por ciento de descuento en tours con la
agencia del hotel.   **8.** No, la estancia mínima es de dos noches.

Los mandatos formales . . . .

A. **Consejos para el viaje.** **1.** Reserve una habitación. **2.** Pregunte si hay aire acondicionado. **3.** Haga las maletas. **4.** Lea una guía turística. **5.** No lleve muchas cosas. **6.** Pague con tarjeta de crédito. **7.** Deje su casa cerrada. **8.** Llegue al aeropuerto dos horas antes del vuelo.

B. **Ya nos vamos.** **1.** Pongan los boletos en el bolsillo de mi impermeable. **2.** Apaguen la luz. **3.** No dejen el radio encendido. **4.** Pidan un taxi. **5.** Traigan las maletas a la puerta. **6.** Busquen el correo de hoy. **7.** Saquen la basura. **8.** No discutan más.

C. **Hablando con el botones.** **1.** Sí, cuélguelos. **2.** Sí, ciérrelas. **3.** Sí, póngalo. **4.** Sí, apáguela. **5.** Sí, tráigalas. **6.** Sí, llámela. **7.** Sí, búsquelo.

D. **Contradicciones.** **1.** Sí, vístanse./No, no se vistan. **2.** Sí, pónganselos./No, no se los pongan. **3.** Sí, siéntense a la mesa./No, no se sienten a la mesa. **4.** Sí, prepárenselo./No, no se lo preparen. **5.** Sí, quédense en la cocina./No, no se queden en la cocina. **6.** Sí, váyanse./No, no se vayan.

El subjuntivo con deseos y emociones. . . . .

A. **1.** es **2.** dé **3.** tenga **4.** suba **5.** haya **6.** hagan **7.** traigan **8.** firmemos
B. **¡Qué hotel!** **1.** esté **2.** devuelvan **3.** explique **4.** esté **5.** es **6.** baje **7.** demos **8.** llamen **9.** permitan
C. **Para hablar en el hotel.** **1.** firmen **2.** traiga **3.** apaguen **4.** vengan **5.** despierten **6.** haga **7.** recomienden **8.** haya
D. *Answers will vary.*

El subjuntivo expresiones de duda y negación. . . . .

A. **¿Cómo es este hotel?** **1.** ¿Piensas que este hotel sea caro?/Sí, pienso que es caro./No, no pienso que sea caro. **2.** ¿Dudan Uds. que este hotel tenga piscina?/Sí, dudamos que tenga piscina./No, no dudamos que tiene piscina. **3.** ¿Cree Ud. que este hotel esté cerca del centro?/Sí, creo que está cerca del centro./No, no creo que esté cerca del centro. **4.** ¿Es cierto que este hotel dé descuentos?/Sí, es cierto que da descuentos./No, no es cierto que dé descuentos. **5.** ¿Es posible que este hotel incluya el desayuno en el precio de la habitación?/Sí, es posible que incluya el desayuno en el precio de la habitación./No, no es posible que incluya el desayuno en el precio de la habitación.
B. **Primer día en Puerto Vallarta.** **1.** ...sirvan el desayuno en el patio. **2.** ...todas las habitaciones estén alquiladas. **3.** ...organicen bailes todas las noches. **4.** ...el hotel tenga doce restaurantes. **5.** ...pasen películas nuevas todos los días. **6.** ...podamos llevarnos las toallas.

Lección 10

Las diversiones

Conversación. . . . .

A. **Vamos a salir.** **1.** a menos que **2.** queden **3.** pueda **4.** para **5.** llames **6.** el teatro **7.** querrá **8.** Tan pronto como

El futuro. . . . .

A. **Pensando en el futuro.** **1.** Alexandra pintará una obra maestra. **2.** Yo actuaré en una película. **3.** Carlos y Francisca trabajarán en el teatro. **4.** Tú serás un músico famoso. **5.** Tú y yo viviremos de nuestro arte. **6.** Ustedes compondrán canciones.
B. **¡Salgamos!** **1.** haremos **2.** Iremos **3.** escogeré **4.** sacarás **5.** Saldremos **6.** vendrán **7.** escucharán **8.** podremos
C. **¿Cómo serán las cosas aquí?** **1.** Irá todo el mundo al teatro. **2.** Pondrán obras muy interesantes. **3.** Serán caras las entradas. **4.** El periódico tendrá una buena cartelera. **5.** Los teatros estarán en el centro. **6.** Las taquillas abrirán por la tarde.

El subjuntivo con algunas expresiones adverbiales . . . .

A. Oraciones. **1.** Te daré el dinero a menos que no lo necesites. Te daré el dinero con tal de que me lo devuelvas. Te daré el dinero para que te compres ropa nueva. Te daré el dinero sin que me lo pidas.
2. Hablaremos con los Martínez sin que nadie lo sepa. Hablaremos con los Martínez para que comprendan el asunto. Hablaremos con los Martínez antes de que Adela los llame. Hablaremos con los Martínez a menos que no quieran escucharnos. **3.** Yo te ayudo con las matemáticas con tal de que te esfuerces. Yo te ayudo con las matemáticas para que saques una buena nota. Yo te ayudo con las matemáticas a menos que no quieras. Yo te ayudo con las matemáticas antes de que el profesor dé el examen. **4.** Vamos al museo de arte a menos que los chicos prefieran hacer otra cosa. Vamos al museo de arte sin que Carolina lo sepa. Vamos al museo de arte para que los chicos vean las obras maestras. Vamos al museo de arte con tal de que no sea demasiado tarde.

B. Hablando de diversiones. *Answers will vary.*

El subjuntivo con otras expresiones adverbiales. . . . .

A. Siempre así. **1.** Lloraré cuando vea esa película. / Lloré cuando vi esa película. **2.** Esperaré hasta que lleguen los chicos. / Esperé hasta que llegaron los chicos. **3.** Saldrán tan pronto como termine la función. / Salieron tan pronto como terminó la función. **4.** Ayudarás a Pablo aunque sea difícil. / Ayudaste a Pablo aunque fue difícil.

B. ¡Teatro! *Answers will vary.*

Las preposiciones *para* y *por* . . . .

A. **1.** para **2.** para **3.** por **4.** por **5.** para **6.** por **7.** para **8.** para **9.** por **10.** Por **11.** para **12.** para **13.** Por **14.** por

Los pronombres con preposiciones . . . .

A. **1.** Sí, son para ti. **2.** Sí, hice esto por ellos. **3.** Sí, va (al cine) conmigo. **4.** Sí, pagué mucho por él. **5.** Sí, influyó mucho en ella. **6.** Sí, irá sin nosotros.

B. Éste sí, el otro no. **1.** Para ella, sí. Para él, no. **2.** Contigo, sí. Conmigo, no. **3.** Con él, sí. Con ella, no. **4.** De mí, sí. De ti, no. **5.** A ellas, sí. A ellos, no. **6.** En mí, sí. En ellos, no.

Answer Key to the Laboratory Manual

Lección preliminar

¡Saludos!

Conversación

A. **1.** a   **2.** a   **3.** b   **4.** c   **5.** a

Cultura

1. Estados   **2.** capital   **3.** ciudad   **4.** español   **5.** país   **6.** playas   **7.** hay   **8.** norte
9. tropicales

Alfabeto

C. Diphthongs.   **1.** c<u>ua</u>tro   **2.** m<u>uy</u>   **3.** d<u>ie</u>z   **4.** ad<u>ió</u>s   **5.** tr<u>ei</u>nta   **6.** n<u>ue</u>ve

Números 0–99

A.   **1.** Evita González: 9-45-98-87   **2.** Fernán Molina: 2-12-30-60   **3.** Samuel Ordóñez: 5-62-09-14
4. Jacinto Tello: 7-32-56-29   **5.** Luisa Osorio: 4-44-19-15

Lección 1

La clase y las presentaciones

Conversación

B. Usted: Buenos días. Me llamo *your name*. ¿Cómo se llama usted?
Srta. Peña: Me llamo Isabel Peña.
Usted: Mucho gusto, señorita. (Encantado/Encantada, señorita. *is also possible.*)
Srta. Peña: El gusto es mío.

Pronouns

A. **1.** Ella es de España.   **2.** Ellas son cantantes.   **3.** Ustedes son de Puerto Rico.   **4.** Nosotros somos
estudiantes.   **5.** Él es cubano.   **6.** Ellos son de México.

Ser

A. ¿Quiénes son estas personas?
1. Tú eres turista. Eres de España.   **2.** Julio y Marcos son actores. Son de Colombia.   **3.** Yo soy estudiante. Soy de los Estados Unidos.   **4.** María y Luisa son doctoras. Son de Cuba.   **5.** Tú y yo somos
compañeros. Somos de México.   **6.** Vicente es programador. Es de Nicaragua.

El salón de clase

A. **Número 3.** No, no es el televisor. Es la luz.   **Número 4.** No, no son las puertas. Son las
ventanas.   **Número 5.** No, no es la ventana. Es la puerta.   **Número 6.** No, no es la pizarra. Es la
computadora.   **Número 7.** No, no son los escritorios. Son los libros.   **Número 8.** No, no es la calculadora. Es el reloj.

Dictado

A. Buenas tardes. Me llamo Víctor Romero. Soy mexicano. Soy de la ciudad de México. Yo soy programador
de computadoras. Me gustan mucho los deportes. Me gusta jugar fútbol. ¿Te gustan los deportes? ¡Vamos a
jugar fútbol!

Lección 2

La familia y las descripciones

C. **True/False.**
1. C **2.** F **3.** F **4.** C **5.** F **6.** F **7.** C **8.** F

La familia . . . .

A. **1.** No, la familia de Pablito Ortega es bastante grande. **2.** Sí, los abuelos Linares son de España. **3.** No, la madre de Pablito es profesora. **4.** Sí, los tíos son inteligentes. **5.** No, las primas son muy simpáticas.

Dictado . . . .

A. La familia de Pablito Ortega es bastante grande. Hay abuelos, tíos y primas. La familia de Pablito es de México, pero los abuelos Linares, los padres de la madre de Pablito, son de España. Los abuelos no trabajan. Ayudan con los niños. Los padres de Pablito son profesores. Enseñan en la universidad. El tío Antonio estudia medicina y el tío Marcos trabaja en una oficina. Los dos tíos son muy inteligentes y muy trabajadores. La tía Ana María es artista. Trabaja en casa. Las primas de Pablito, Sara y Paula, son muy simpáticas. Son buenas estudiantes también.

B. **Translation.**
Pablito Ortega's family is rather large. There are grandparents, aunts and uncles, and cousins. Pablito's family is from Mexico, but the Linares grandmother and grandfather, the parents of Pablito's mother, are from Spain. The grandparents don't work. They help with the children. Pablito's parents are professors (teachers). They teach at the university. Uncle Antonio is studying medicine and Uncle Marcos works in an office. Both uncles are very intelligent and very hard-working. Aunt Ana María is an artist. She works at home. Pablito's cousins, Sara and Paula, are very nice. They are good students too.

Descripciones . . . .

A. **1.** Tesesa es morena. **2.** Los abuelos son viejos. **3.** El libro es fácil. **4.** La biblioteca es pequeña. **5.** Mis primas son solteras.

B. **1.** Sí, escucho bien. **2.** No, no desayuno con los compañeros. **3.** No, los estudiantes no bailan. **4.** No, la profesora no maneja un coche. **5.** No, no participo en los deportes.

Ser y estar . . . .

A. **Mi familia.** **1.** Mis padres son simpáticos. **2.** Yo estoy ocupada. **3.** Mis hermanos menores están cansados. **4.** Mi abuela está enferma. **5.** Mi abuelo está preocupado. **6.** Mis hermanas están contentas. **7.** Mis primos son divertidos. **8.** Mi tía Alicia está enojada.

B. **Lógico o ilógico.** **1.** ilógico **2.** ilógico **3.** lógico **4.** ilógico **5.** ilógico **6.** lógico

Lección 3

Las comidas

Conversación . . . .

A. *(Answers may vary slightly.)* **1.** Lucía cree que hay muchas cosas buenas en el menú. **2.** Lucía va a comer una sopa de cebolla. **3.** Después va a comer pollo, papas y verduras. **4.** Desea una ensalada de lechuga y tomates. **5.** Va a tomar agua mineral con la comida. **6.** El restaurante prepara tortas. (Preparan tortas en el restaurante.) **7.** No hay cuchillo en la mesa de Lucía. **8.** Después de la comida, Lucía toma café.

El verbo *ir*

A. **1.** ¿Vas a la biblioteca? **2.** ¿Voy a la cafetería? **3.** ¿Van al gimnasio? **4.** ¿Vamos a la oficina? **5.** ¿Van a la universidad?

B. **El fin de semana.** **1.** Yo voy a estudiar. **2.** Mi mamá va a cocinar. **3.** Mis amigos van a jugar al fútbol. **4.** Carmen va a comprar una computadora. **5.** Tú vas a escuchar música.

El presente de los verbos *-er/-ir*

A. **1.** Sí, come enchiladas. **2.** No, no conozco a Marta. **3.** Sí, aprendo español. **4.** No, no recibimos cartas. **5.** Sí, comparto la comida con los amigos. **6.** No, no debemos ir a la biblioteca.

La *a* personal

A. **1.** Mis amigos ven un programa de televisión. **2.** María ve a sus tíos. **3.** Rosario y Sara ven al mesero. **4.** Eduardo ve la nueva película. **5.** Nosotros vemos a Daniela. **6.** Tú ves a tus compañeros.

Los días

A. **1.** Mañana es domingo. **2.** Mañana es viernes. **3.** Mañana es miércoles. **4.** Mañana es lunes. **5.** Mañana es viernes.

Los meses

A. **1.** No, es en agosto. **2.** No, es en junio. **3.** No, es en noviembre. **4.** No, es en abril. **5.** No, es en febrero.

Dictado

A. El sábado por la noche mis amigos y yo vamos a comer en mi casa. Cada uno va a preparar algo y vamos a compartir los platos que hacemos. Yo debo preparar una ensalada grande. Marta y Luisa compran un pollo. Van a preparar un pollo asado. Carlos y Raúl compran papas. ¡Me gustan las papas fritas y Carlos y Raúl saben preparar papas fritas deliciosas! Isabel va a comprar platos de papel y tenedores, cuchillos y cucharas de plástico. Rosario, una nueva estudiante mexicana de nuestra universidad, va a preparar unos platos mexicanos: chilaquiles y enchiladas. Creo que vamos a comer muy bien.

B. *(Sample answer)*
On Saturday night my friends and I are going to eat at my house. Each one is going to prepare something and we are going to share the dishes that we make. I'm supposed to prepare a big salad. Marta and Luisa are buying a chicken. They're going to prepare a roast chicken. Carlos and Raúl are buying potatoes. I like French fried potatoes and Carlos and Raúl know how to prepare delicious French fries! Isabel is going to buy paper plates and plastic forks, knives, and spoons. Rosario, a new Mexican student at our university, is going to prepare some Mexican dishes: chilaquiles and enchiladas. I think we're going to eat very well.

Lección 4

Las actividades diarias

C. **1.** Felipe se levanta temprano (a las seis y media) los lunes. **2.** Felipe tiene historia a las ocho. **3.** El profesor Dávila da mucho trabajo. **4.** Los libros son muy interesantes. **5.** Felipe almuerza a la una.

Los adjetivos posesivos

A. **¡Listos para la clase!** **1.** Martín tiene su bolígrafo. **2.** Todos los estudiantes tienen sus cuadernos. **3.** Nosotros tenemos nuestros libros. **4.** Tú tienes tu calculadora. **5.** Yo tengo mi horario. **6.** Tú y yo tenemos nuestras computadoras.

B. Para ser preciso.   **1.** La foto del niño.   **2.** El restaurante del señor Morales.   **3.** El carro de la hermana de Carlos.   **4.** El examen del profesor Sánchez.   **5.** Las casa de los vecinos.   **6.** Las verduras del mercado.

Verbos con cambios radicales e → ie, o → ue

A. ¿Qué hacen hoy?   **1.** Tú y yo almorzamos en un restaurante.   **2.** Margarita almuerza en casa.   **3.** Yo vuelvo a la universidad.   **4.** Papá y mamá quieren salir.   **5.** Tú empiezas a estudiar.   **6.** Mi perro duerme.

B. Yo también.   **1.** Yo tengo prisa.   **2.** Yo también me pongo el suéter.   **3.** Yo también hago la tarea.   **4.** Yo también traigo vinos.   **5.** Yo también salgo hoy.   **6.** Yo también digo «Buenos días».

Los verbos reflexivos

A. La familia Durán.   **1.** Papá se afeita.   **2.** Mis hermanitos se divierten en el jardín.   **3.** Yo me pongo la ropa.   **4.** Mamá se sienta a desayunar.   **5.** Mi hermana y yo nos peinamos.   **6.** Mi hermano Carlos se queda en la cama.   **7.** Mis abuelos se enojan con Carlos.   **8.** Todos nosotros nos vamos a las diez.

La hora

A. ¿A qué hora es?   **1.** no   **2.** sí   **3.** no   **4.** no   **5.** sí   **6.** sí   **7.** no   **8.** sí
B. ¡Escuche, por favor!   **1.** c   **2.** b   **3.** d   **4.** b   **5.** a   **6.** d   **7.** c   **8.** a

Lección 5

La salud y el cuerpo

Conversación

B.   **1.** F   **2.** C   **3.** ¿?   **4.** F   **5.** F   **6.** C   **7.** F   **8.** ¿?
C. ¡Un accidente!   **1.** cabeza   **2.** los brazos   **3.** el cuello   **4.** la nariz   **5.** los hombros   **6.** estómago   **7.** las piernas

Verbos con cambios radicales e → i

A. ¡Ay, qué catarro!   **1.** Yo pido medicina.   **2.** Nosotros pedimos medicina.   **3.** Tú pides medicina.   **4.** Pablo pide medicina.   **5.** Uds. piden medicina.   **6.** Carlos y yo pedimos medicina.

Expresiones con *tener*

A.   **1.** Tiene prisa.   **2.** Tienes dolor de cabeza.   **3.** Tengo miedo de verlo.   **4.** Sí, tenemos hambre.   **5.** Sí, ya tiene seis años.   **6.** No, todos tienen frío.

El presente progresivo

A. ¡Esta gripe no termina!   **1.** Sí, estoy tomando aspirinas.   **2.** Sí, me está sirviendo un té caliente.   **3.** Sí, estoy estornudando mucho.   **4.** Sí, estoy tomando antibióticos.   **5.** Sí, estoy leyendo revistas.   **6.** Sí, me están trayendo la tarea.

Los pronombres de complemento directo

A.   **1.** Sí, te acompaño.   **2.** Sí, me comprendes.   **3.** No, no te recuerdo.   **4.** No, no me conoces.   **5.** Sí, te ayudo.   **6.** No, no te espero.
B.   **1.** Sí, los acompañamos.   **2.** Sí, nos comprenden.   **3.** No, no los recordamos.   **4.** No, no nos conocen.   **5.** Sí, las ayudamos.   **6.** No, no las esperamos.
C.   **1.** ¿Por qué no la preparas?   **2.** ¿Por qué no los tomas?   **3.** ¿Por qué no lo comprendes?   **4.** ¿Por qué no las estudias?   **5.** ¿Por qué no lo manejas?   **6.** ¿Por qué no las abres?

Dictado

A. Yo me llamo Carlota y vivo en la residencia de la universidad. Tengo dos compañeras María y Clara. Las dos tienen gripe ahora. María tiene fiebre y tose todo el día y Clara estornuda mucho y no respira bien. Yo tengo que ayudarlas, porque no pueden salir. Voy a la farmacia por ellas y pido aspirinas y vitaminas. María y Clara no comen mucho, pero les traigo sopa y pan. Aaa-chís. ¿Qué es esto? Ahora estoy estornudando yo. Y tengo dolor de cabeza y de espalda, y estoy un poco mareada. ¡No! ¡Yo me estoy enfermando también! ¿Quién va a cuidarme a mí?

Lección 6

En la tienda de ropa

Conversación

C. 1. C 2. F 3. C 4. F 5. C 6. C

Adjetivos y pronombres demostrativos

A. 1. ¿Ése? No tanto. Me gusta más el otro. 2. ¿Ésas? No tanto. Me gustan más las otras. 3. ¿Ésa? No tanto. Me gusta más la otra. 4. ¿Ésos? No tanto. Me gustan más los otros. 5. ¿Ése? No tanto. Me gusta más el otro.

Imperfecto

A. Antes las vacaciones eran diferentes. 1. Ahora no. Antes iba con la familia. 2. Ahora no. Antes nadábamos en un lago. 3. Ahora no. Antes había otros chicos allí. 4. Ahora no. Antes me ponía un pantalón corto todos los días. 5. Ahora no. Antes dábamos muchos paseos. 6. Ahora no. Antes venían muchos amigos a vernos. 7. Ahora no. Antes teníamos una casa en el campo. 8. Ahora no. Antes invitaba a mis amigos al campo.

Los pronombres de complemento indirecto

A. 1. ¿Le mandas una carta a Roberto? 2. ¿Les mandas un regalo a tus abuelos? 3. ¿Le mandas los cincuenta dólares a Carlota? 4. ¿Les mandas las fotos a tus padres? 5. ¿Le mandas una sudadera a tu hermano menor?
B. 1. c 2. c 3. a 4. b 5. a
C. A nadie le gusta esta ropa. 1. No, no me gustan. 2. No, no nos gustan. 3. No, no les gustan. 4. No, no le gusta. 5. No, no les gusta.
D. Hablando de ropa. 1. No, le parece fea. 2. No, le parece pequeño. 3. Sí, le parecen elegantes. 4. No, les parecen caras. 5. Sí, me parece fantástico.

¡Escuche, por favor!

A. Buscándose un vestido. 1. F 2. C 3. F 4. F 5. C 6. F 7. F 8. F

Lección 7

El hogar y los muebles

Conversación

B. 1. F 2. C 3. C 4. C 5. F 6. C 7. F 8. C 9. F 10. C

Números **145**

A. **En la mueblería.** **1.** 715 **2.** 529 **3.** 180 **4.** 463 **5.** 350 **6.** 190

B. **En el rastro.** **1.** Cierto **2.** Falso **3.** Cierto **4.** Falso **5.** Cierto **6.** Cierto **7.** Cierto
8. Falso **9.** Cierto **10.** Falso

C. **1.** Ya los leí. **2.** Ya la pidió. **3.** Ya la vimos. **4.** Ya la compraron. **5.** Ya las repitieron.
6. Ya los serví.

D. **1.** Mamá no durmió bien. **2.** Yo no salí. **3.** Mis amigos no se divirtieron. **4.** Yo no fui al
cine. **5.** Tú no contestaste la pregunta. **6.** Los otros estudiantes no leyeron mucho.

E. **1.** Yo comí tanto como Pablo. **2.** Los chicos jugaron tanto como tú. **3.** Carlos leyó tanto como
yo. **4.** Nosotros entendimos tanto como Marcos. **5.** Las chicas durmieron tanto como tú. **6.** Los
hombres corrieron tanto como las mujeres.

La combinación de dos complimentos . . . .

A. **1.** Sí, se la presté. **2.** Sí, se lo vendí. **3.** Sí, te los di. **4.** Sí, se lo reparé. **5.** Sí, se las
enseñé. **6.** Sí, se lo pedí. **7.** Sí, se los regalé. **8.** Sí, te la devolví.

Lección 8

De viaje

Conversación . . . .

A. **1.** no **2.** sí **3.** sí **4.** no **5.** sí

Dictado parcial . . . .

A. **1.** llegaron **2.** vivían **3.** tenían **4.** eran **5.** más **6.** países **7.** lengua
8. conocían **9.** llevaron **10.** empezó **11.** eran **12.** Construyeron **13.** altos
14. mejores

El pretérito de los verbos irregulares . . . .

A. **1.** Fuimos al aeropuerto. **2.** Fui al aeropuerto. **3.** Fue al aeropuerto. (/) **4.** Fueron al
aeropuerto. **5.** Fue al aeropuerto.

B. **1.** Sí, ayer hice las maletas. **2.** Sí, ayer hicieron las maletas. **3.** Sí, ayer hicimos las maletas.
4. Sí, ayer hiciste las maletas. **5.** Sí, ayer hizo las maletas.

C. **1.** No, vine tarde. **2.** No, vinieron tarde. **3.** No, vinimos tarde. **4.** No, vino tarde. **5.** No,
viniste tarde.

D. **1.** Tuve que hacerlo. **2.** Tuvieron que hacerlo. **3.** Tuvimos que hacerlo. **4.** Tuviste que
hacerlo. **5.** Tuvo que hacerlo.

Comparaciones de desigualdad . . . .

A. **1.** El viaje en autobús es más largo que el viaje en tren. **2.** Tu maleta grande es más pesada que mi
maleta. **3.** Los comprobantes son menos importantes que los boletos. **4.** El autobús es menos
cómodo que el carro. **5.** El aeropuerto es más grande que la estación de trenes.

B. **1.** Paula es más simpática que María. Paula es la más simpática. **2.** José es más gordo que Carlos. José es
el más gordo. **3.** Laura es más popular que Ana. Laura es la más popular. **4.** Nicolás es más inteligente que Jorge. Nicolás es el más inteligente. **5.** Teresa es más alegre que Lola. Teresa es la más alegre.

Comparaciones de igualdad . . . .

A. **1.** Bueno, tenemos tantas maletas como Ud. **2.** Bueno, hacemos tantos viajes como Ud. **3.** Bueno,
facturamos tanto equipaje como Ud. **4.** Bueno, resolvemos tantos problemas como Ud. **5.** Bueno,
cambiamos tantos pesos como Ud.

Lección 9

En el hotel

Conversación . . . .

¿Cierto o falso? 1. C   2. F   3. C   4. F   5. C   6. F   7. C   8. C   9. F   10. F

El subjuntivo con deseos . . . .

A. 1. subjunctive   2. nonsubjunctive   3. subjunctive   4. subjunctive   5. subjunctive
6. nonsubjunctive

Los mandatos . . . .

C. 1. ¿Por qué no? Vaya Ud.   2. ¿Por qué no? Vengan Uds.   3. ¿Por qué no? Espere Ud.   4. ¿Por qué no? Coman Uds.   5. ¿Por qué no? Suba Ud.   6. ¿Por qué no? Estudien Uds.   7. ¿Por qué no? Juegue Ud.   8. ¿Por qué no? Vuelvan Uds.   9. ¿Por qué no? Descanse Ud.   10. ¿Por qué no? Viajen Uds.

B. 1. Sí, cómo no. Levántese Ud.   2. Sí, cómo no. Váyanse Uds.   3. Sí, cómo no. Acuéstese Ud.
4. Sí, cómo no. Quédense Uds.   5. Sí, cómo no. Lávese Ud.   6. Sí, cómo no. Aféitense Uds.

C. 1. No, no se vaya Ud.   2. No, no se preocupen Uds.   3. No, no se duerma Ud.   4. No, no se maquillen Uds.   5. No, no se quede Ud.   6. No, no se sirvan Uds.

El subjuntivo con deseos . . . .

B. 1. Es necesario que dobles a la izquierda.   2. Quiero que apagues la televisión.   3. No quiero que te vayas.   4. Me alegro de que saques fotos.   5. Espero que subas.   6. Sé que sabes el precio.
7. Siento que tengas miedo.   8. Creo que comprendes.

El subjuntivo con dudas . . . .

A. 1. Dudo que venga.   2. No creo que estén listos.   3. Es posible que se queden a cenar.   4. Creo que tenemos vino.   5. No es cierto que nos traigan regalos.

B. 1. No pienso que la camarera venga dos veces al día.   2. No es cierto que tengan un restaurante excelente.   3. No estoy segura de que todo el mundo se divierta aquí.   4. No es verdad que los precios son moderados aquí.   5. No creo que todo funcione en nuestro cuarto.

C. 1. ¿Quieres que llame a la camarera?   2. ¿Cuántas toallas quieres que traiga la camarera?   3. ¿A qué hora quieres que nos despierten?   4. ¿Prefieres que yo ponga las maletas en la mesa o en la silla?
5. ¿Crees que el restaurante esté abierto todavía?   6. ¿Es necesario que cambien la bombilla del baño?   7. ¿Dónde prefieres que comamos?   8. ¿Quieres que yo escoja una película para esta noche?

Lección 10

Las diversiones

Conversación . . . .

B. 1. C   2. F   3. C   4. F   5. F   6. C   7. C   8. F

Las preposiciones *para* y *por* . . . .

A. 1. b   2. a   3. a   4. b   5. a

B. Dictado.   1. Velázquez   2. El Escorial   3. Quito   4. San Juan de Teotihuacán   5. Sevilla
6. Cuzco   7. Frida Kahlo

El futuro.. 147

A. **1.** No sé si saldré. **2.** No sé si volverán. **3.** No sé si vendrán. **4.** No sé si subiremos. **5.** No sé si me esperará. **6.** No sé si te invitará.

B. **1.** No, regresarán mañana. **2.** No, estudiaré mañana. **3.** No, saldremos mañana. **4.** No, hará la cena mañana. **5.** No, pondrán una película nueva mañana. **6.** No, trabajarás mañana.

El subjuntivo con algunas expresiones adverbiales ....

A. **1.** Sacaré las entradas para que tú veas la película.
Sacaré las entradas para que los chicos vean la película.
Sacaré las entradas para que María vea la película.

2. No me voy de aquí antes que usted hable con el profesor.
No me voy de aquí antes que tú hables con el profesor.
No me voy de aquí antes que ustedes hablen con el profesor.

3. Nadie sale sin que yo quiera.
Nadie sale sin que tú quieras.
Nadie sale sin que nuestros padres quieran.

4. Nos veremos con tal que tú llegues por la mañana.
Nos veremos con tal que ustedes lleguen por la mañana.
Nos veremos con tal que usted llegue por la mañana.

5. Terminaré el trabajo para que nosotros podamos salir.
Terminaré el trabajo para que ustedes puedan salir.
Terminaré el trabajo para que tú puedas salir.

6. No lo vamos a hacer sin que tú tengas el permiso de papá.
No lo vamos a hacer sin que yo tenga el permiso de papá.
No lo vamos a hacer sin que nuestros hermanos tengan el permiso de papá.

7. Vamos a cenar antes que los chicos vayan al concierto.
Vamos a cenar antes que Paula vaya al concierto.
Vamos a cenar antes que tú vayas al concierto.

8. Iremos con tal que Marta no esté muy ocupada.
Iremos con tal que mis hermanos no estén muy ocupados.
Iremos con tal que Pedro no esté muy ocupado.

El subjuntivo con otras expresiones adverbiales..........................

A. **1.** Lo haré cuando pueda. **2.** Lo hará cuando pueda. **3.** Lo haremos cuando podamos. **4.** Lo harás cuando puedas. **5.** Lo harán cuando puedan. **6.** Lo harán cuando puedan.

B. **1.** Saldré cuando tenga tiempo. **2.** Saldrás cuando tengas tiempo. **3.** Los chicos saldrán cuando tengan tiempo. **4.** Tú y yo saldremos cuando tengamos tiempo. **5.** Francisco saldrá cuando tenga tiempo. **6.** Ustedes saldrán cuando tengan tiempo.

Los pronombres con preposiciones..

A. **1.** A ella, sí. A él, no. **2.** A ti, sí. A ellos, no. **3.** A ellas, sí. A ellos, no. **4.** A ustedes, sí. A ellas, no. **5.** A ellos, sí. A ellas no.

B. **1.** A ella, no. A él, sí. **2.** A él, no. A mí, sí. **3.** A ellos, no. A nosotros, sí. **4.** A ella, no. A ellos, sí. **5.** A él, no. A ella, sí.